Justice, Mercy and Humility

Justice, Mercy and Humility

The Papers of the Micah Network
International Consultation on Integral
Mission and the Poor (2001)

Edited by Tim Chester

PATERNOSTER PRESS

Paternoster Press is an imprint of Authentic Media,
P.O. Box 300, Carlisle, Cumbria, CA3 0QS, UK
and
P.O. Box 1047, Waynesboro, GA 30830-2047, USA

Website: www.paternoster-publishing.com

British Library Cataloguing in Publication Data
A catalogue record for this book is available from the British Library

ISBN 1-84227-162-8

Cover Design by FourNineZero
Typeset by WestKey Ltd, Falmouth, Cornwall
Printed in Great Britain by Cox and Wyman, Reading, Berkshire

Contents

Part Two: Integral Mission and the Poor

Part Three: Integral Mission and the Church

Part Four: Integral Mission, Advocacy and Lifestyle

Contributors

Douglas Boyle

Douglas Boyle is Mission Director of the Assemblies of God in Kazakstan and Executive Director of Teen Challenge, Kazakstan.

Steve Bradbury

Steve Bradbury is the Director of TEAR Australia and Chair of the Micah Network.

Tim Chester

Tim Chester is part of a church planting team in Sheffield, UK. He was formerly the Research and Policy Director of Tearfund UK. He is visiting lecturer in Christian Community Development at Redcliffe College, UK, and author of *Awakening to a World of Need: The Recovery of Evangelical Social Concern* (Leicester, UK: IVP, 1993).

Janet Cornwall

Janet Cornwall has been Project Co-ordinator for Servants to Asia's Urban Poor in Cambodia since 1995. Her training is in medicine and she has also worked in South Africa.

Tim Costello

Tim Costello is Director of the Urban Mission Unit, Melbourne, Australia, and President of the Baptist Union of Australia. A former mayor of a local council, he is currently engaged in holistic ministry among drug addicts and sex workers in Melbourne.

Saul and Pilar Cruz

Saul and Pilar Cruz are the Co-directors of Armonia Ministries, which serves poor communities in both urban and rural contexts in Mexico. Saul is a psychologist, family therapist and university lecturer by profession and Pilar is a lecturer.

Robert Guerrero

Robert Guerrero is the Pastor of Iglesia Comunitaria Cristiana, a local church working in a poor area of the Dominican Republic. He is the General Co-ordinator of the El Camino Network and a founding member of the Network of Churches and Ministries for Integral Mission in Dominican Republic.

Gary A Haugen

Gary Haugen worked in the civil rights division of the US Department of Justice and was Director of the UN genocide investigation in Rwanda. He is currently President of the International Justice Mission, Washington DC. He is the author of *Good News about Injustice* (Downers Grove, Illinois: InterVarsity Press, 1999).

Susan Jack

Susan Jack has worked for over seven years in Cambodia for Servants to Asia's Urban Poor as child health advisor.

John Wesley Kabango

John Wesley Kabango co-ordinates rural development activities and encourages churches to implement integral mission in the four dioceses of the Episcopal Church of Rwanda for the Rural Development Interdiocesan Service.

Bishop Peter Kitula

Peter Kitula is Bishop of the Diocese of Mara and Ukerewe of the Africa Inland Church, Tanzania.

Peter Kuzmiĉ

Peter Kuzmiĉ is the Founding Director of the Evangelical Theological Faculty, Osiejk, Croatia, and Toms Distinguished Professor at Gordon-Conwell Theological Seminary, Boston, USA. He has been actively engaged in peacemaking, interethnic and interreligious reconciliation initiatives in the Balkans. He is Founding President of Agape, a Christian relief organization.

Archbishop Donald Mtetemala

Donald Mtetemala is the Anglican Archbishop of Tanzania.

Lorraine Muchaneta

Lorraine Muchaneta is the Co-ordinator of church-based projects for the Family AIDS Caring Trust, Zimbabwe.

Oswaldo E Munguía

Oswaldo Munguía is Co-founder and Executive Director of MOPAWI, Honduras, where he has worked for over 16 years.

C René Padilla

René Padilla is the Director of the Kairos Foundation in Buenos Aires, President of the Micah Network and International President of Tearfund UK. He has been a prominent advocate of integral mission through his many writings and his participation in the major evangelical mission consultations over the past 30 years.

Ann Pettifor

Ann Pettifor was the Director of the Jubilee 2000 Coalition. She is now the Programme Co-ordinator for Jubilee Plus, which provides information and analysis on international debt. Jubilee Plus is a programme of the think-tank the New Economics Foundation.

Tiago Sampaio

Tiago Sampaio is Project Co-ordinator for the community development and relief programme of the Evangelical Church of Guinea-Bissau.

CB Samuel

CB Samuel is a Bible teacher on wholism in mission and a mentor of younger leaders. He was previously the director of EFICOR (Evangelical Fellowship of India Commission on Relief), India.

Tom and Christine Sine

Tom Sine is an author and consultant in futures research. Christine Aroney-Sine is a consultant in international healthcare. Tom spent several years in community development in Haiti and Christine directed the healthcare ministry for YWAM's Mercy Ships. Tom is Adjunct Professor at Fuller Theological Seminary, California, where Christine also teaches on urban poverty.

Elaine Storkey

Elaine Storkey is the President of Tearfund UK, and an academic, broadcaster and writer. She is currently Director of Apologetics for the Zacharias Trust.

Alfonso Wieland

Alfonso Wieland is a lawyer specializing in human rights. He is Executive Director of Peace and Hope, a Christian organization in Peru that works on issues of social justice. He is a member of the Micah Network Co-ordinating Group.

Introducing Integral Mission

Tim Chester

Daniel was born in Jalalpa, one of the many slums of Mexico City. His father abandoned the family and his mother turned to drink and to men. To provide for himself and his siblings, Daniel got a job running orders for the tradesmen who operate outside Mexico's prisons. With a bribe to the guard, children like Daniel supply alcohol, cigarettes and even women to the inmates. In time Daniel was caught and sent to a young offenders' institution. The judge ordered that on his release he should not live with his mother. But after a short time with his grandmother, he returned to his mother to care for his siblings. One day his half-blind brother was killed in a road accident. Enslaved by his mother and full of guilt about the death of his brother, Daniel was left distraught and suicidal.

What hope is there for the likes of Daniel? What hope is there for the thousands of slum communities around the world? What does the mission of the church look like in such situations? It was to consider such questions that 140 Christian leaders, theologians and practitioners from 50 countries met in Oxford, UK, in September 2001, under the auspices of the Micah Network.

It was natural for the Micah Network to make integral mission the theme of its first international consultation. A commitment to the task of integral mission among the poor is what defines the network. The term 'consultation' was deliberately chosen to express a commitment to a participatory process of mutual learning and decision making. The consultation produced the *Micah Declaration* with a declaration resolution group made up of René Padilla (Chair), Melba Maggay, Dewi Hughes and Tim Chester. The aim of the declaration was to describe the identity of the Micah Network, but also to call the wider church to the task of integral mission among the poor.

The term 'integral mission' comes from the Spanish *'misión integral'* – the term commonly used in Latin America for what others describe as 'holistic ministry', 'Christian development' or 'transformation'. Each of these terms has its merits and its weaknesses. 'Holistic' has in recent years become widely used with quite different connotations from those intended by advocates of integral mission. Because of the dominance of economics in many people's thinking, 'development' runs the risk of implying that wealthy countries are more developed and therefore superior to poorer countries. The problem with the term 'transformation' is that it can mean anything and therefore means nothing. It allows people to undertake activities in the name of mission that exclude social involvement or, more commonly, proclamation. Each of these terms contributes something, but none quite does the job on its own. The *Micah Declaration* uses them all, but 'integral mission' was adopted as the central term. The *Micah Declaration* defines it as follows:

> Integral mission or holistic transformation is the proclamation and demonstration of the gospel. It is not simply that evangelism and social involvement are to be done alongside

each other. Rather, in integral mission our proclamation has social consequences as we call people to love and repentance in all areas of life and our social involvement has evangelistic consequences as we bear witness to the transforming grace of Jesus Christ.

The declaration group chose the wording of this definition with care. We wanted to retain the idea that proclamation and social involvement are distinct activities. We feared that when they are fused into one entity one or other soon falls away. Furthermore, while good social involvement involves harnessing the capabilities, resources and energies of a community, the proclamation of the gospel addresses us in our total helplessness.

But to say that proclamation and social involvement are distinct is not to say they can operate apart from one another. As the *Micah Declaration* says, 'It is not simply that evangelism and social involvement are to be done alongside each other.' According to the Oxford English Dictionary 'integrated' means 'made up of parts', but 'integral' means 'of, or necessary to the completeness of, a whole'. Integral mission recognizes that proclamation and social involvement are necessary components of the mission or task of the church.

It is a basic rule of hermeneutics that texts make sense only in their context. The same is true of mission. Our text – the message we proclaim – will be interpreted by the context of our lives and our life together as Christian communities. Proclamation cannot take place apart from a context. The question is whether that context is congruent with the message of transforming grace in Jesus Christ. The context that properly interprets the gospel message is love. In our love for the 'other' – especially the marginalized – we model the grace of God just as Jesus did in his table fellowship with the outcasts of his day. And so the church itself is, in the words of Lesslie Newbigin, 'the hermeneutic of the gospel'.[1]

Thirty years ago the theological struggle for integral mission was the struggle to gain acceptance for the place of social involvement in mission. As René Padilla reminds us, the Lausanne Congress and the *Lausanne Covenant* were key turning points in this process, while the consultations in Grand Rapids, Michigan, in 1982 and Wheaton, Illinois, in 1983 represent its fullest flowering. In some quarters this is still an area of debate. Indeed there are signs of a retrenchment – often in reaction to a few proponents of social action who have lost their theological moorings.

Yet at the same time among a new generation of evangelicals it is the necessity of making evangelism integral that needs to be affirmed. Brought up in a postmodern milieu that sees a commitment to absolute truth as arrogant, this generation hesitates to proclaim the revealed word of God. Many Christians today – particularly in the West – readily assent to social action, but are less sure about proclaiming the liberating truth of the gospel. But a commitment to integral mission is as much a commitment to make evangelism integral with social action as it is to make social action integral with evangelism. What defines the Micah Network is its unfaltering commitment to keep proclamation and demonstration together – and not just together, but integrally related in a total missional response to the poor.

If Grand Rapids and Wheaton represent the fullest expression of a theological commitment to integral mission, this does not mean the debate has stood still. There have been significant developments in the field of

---

[1] Lesslie Newbigin, *The Gospel in a Pluralist Society* (London: SPCK, 1989), 222–33.

integral mission. The context has changed: we live in a significantly more globalized world. And involvement in integral mission has led to a greater understanding of the roles of the poor and the local church in development as well as the need to address the underlying causes of poverty through advocacy for justice.

1. Globalization

Less than two weeks before the consultation convened, terrorists flew two planes into the twin towers of the World Trade Centre in New York and another plane into the Pentagon in Washington DC. Inevitably this historic event and its still-unfolding consequences cast an unexpected shadow over the consultation. During the consultation a letter was sent on behalf of the Micah Network to Western leaders calling on them 'to seek justice not revenge, peace not war'. The *Micah Declaration* – in perhaps its most discussed section – went further, saying:

> We recognize too the symbolic meaning of this act of terrorism. In his day Jesus interpreted the butchery of Pilate against the Galileans as an opportunity to repent. Could it be that this act against the symbols of Western economic and military power is a call to repentance?

This is a reference to Luke 13, where Jesus is told about Galileans whose blood Pilate had mixed with their sacrifices. Jesus replies:

> Do you think that these Galileans were worse sinners than all the other Galileans because they suffered this way? I tell you, no! But unless you repent, you too will all perish. (Lk. 13:2–3)

We did not want to imply in any way that those who died in the attacks on the World Trade Centre and the Pentagon were 'worse sinners' than the rest of us. But we did want to ask whether God was calling us in the West in particular to repent of our complicity in global military and economic policies that are not right.

Globalization is both an economic phenomenon – the spread of a global free market – and a cultural phenomenon – the spread of a global consumer culture. It brings many benefits, creating wealth and opening up societies. But globalization is also creating gross inequalities, over-whelming local cultures and excluding the poor. The unrestricted movement of capital can leave whole communities devastated as production moves elsewhere at short notice in search of lower costs. Political account-ability is eroded by the centralization of power in the hands of the economically powerful, undermining, for example, local efforts at environmental and labour protection.

Globalization is not only a phenomenon. It is also an ideology. The collapse of communism has led to the hegemony of an unchecked free market and its extension into new areas of society. The market is an important tool for a healthy economy, but when the needs of the market override other ethical and social considerations it has become an idol. To feed this global market a global consumer culture is promoted, promising satisfaction and meaning through the purchase of consumer goods. Brands no longer represent products of a reputable quality. Instead they offer an image unrelated to products that carry them, offering an identity and belonging for those who wear them. This too is idolatry.

It is easy to criticize globalization. The challenge for the church is to develop alternatives, both at the macro-level of policies and advocacy and at the micro-level of our lifestyles. In Revelation 18 the Apostle John condemns the unjust economic practices of Babylon/Rome that include trading the 'bodies and souls of men' (Rev. 18:13). He calls on his readers to 'come out of her ... so that you will not share in her sins' (Rev. 18:4). We need to discover what it means for contemporary Christians to 'come out of her'. We need to develop a new sense of what it means for the church to be a countercultural community. As the *Micah Declaration* says:

> Perhaps the most critical social task for the church in our generation is to offer a compelling alternative to the unjust imbalances in the world economic order and the values of its consumer culture.

2. The Poor and the Church of the Poor

We have been learning from our grass-roots involvement with poor communities. We have learned the importance of the participation of the poor in the process of development. We have learned the need for mutual transformation. We have learned that sustainable development is as much about empowerment, the restoration of dignity and attitudinal change as it is about the provision of physical products and services. We have learned that development is time-intensive rather than capital-intensive. We have learned, above all, that development is about building and rebuilding relationships – with God, with others in community and with creation.

It is not just the poor who must be involved in the development process. At the heart of integral mission is the local church. Christian development NGOs (Non-Governmental Organizations) and development practitioners are wrestling with the role of the church in ministry with the poor. We can no longer be content to ape the models of development professionals. The New Testament does not describe development projects or, for that matter, evangelistic initiatives. Its focus is on Christian communities, which are to be distinctive, caring and inclusive. Integral mission is about the church being the church.

There can be no sustainable Christian development that is distinctly Christian without sustainable Christian communities. This means that often the planting of churches that are committed to the inclusion of the poor must be at the heart of integral mission. In an unpublished paper René Padilla has said:

> One of the greatest challenges we Christians have at the threshold of the third millennium is the articulation and practical implementation of an ecclesiology that views the local church, and particularly the church of the poor, as the primary agent of holistic mission.[2]

But work among the poor is also raising new questions about what it means to be church. For some this renewed emphasis on church is greeted with reluctance because their experience of church is far removed from their experience of work among the poor. New Christians from poor communities often find the cultural leap to established churches too great to cross. And so we are being forced to ask afresh what belongs to the gospel and what belongs to our church cultures. We are being forced to ask afresh what defines church. New forms of church are emerging among the poor. Along with these new expressions of church come questions about how they relate to established churches.

---

[2] Cited in Tim Chester, 'Christ's Little Flock: Towards an Ecclesiology of the Cross', *Evangel* 19:1 (Spring 2001), 13.

3. Advocacy

A further way in which the debate about integral mission has moved on is the recognition that work among the poor must embrace work on the causes of their poverty. Often those causes have to do with structural injustice and the abuse of power. Poverty is a product of marginalization and powerlessness. It is the result of oppression. This should be no surprise to those with a biblical doctrine of sin, for sin is deep and pervasive. It is both personal and structural. As Gary Haugen argues, the church is moving into a new frontier of ministry to the poor – the ministry of advocacy. As we move into this arena, we are discovering afresh the Bible's condemnation of social injustice and its call to speak up for the oppressed.

But the debate is not simply *whether* we should do advocacy, but also *how* we should do advocacy. As the *Micah Declaration* confesses, 'too often the church has pursued wealth, success, status and influence'. Advocacy presents us with a subtle form of this temptation. We must beware lest influence becomes an end in itself. We are advocates for and with the poor. And to stand with the poor is to stand with the marginalized and despised. Referring to 1 Corinthians 4:13, CB Samuel told the consultation:

> If you choose to be irrelevant you are not out of touch. You are where most of the world is. The poor of the world are not relevant. When we become the scum of the world we become what the poor already are.

We follow a Lord who exercised his lordship through service, whose strength lay in his weakness, whose glory was revealed in his shame, whose triumph was won through his defeat. In our advocacy we do not simply pit

our influence against the influence of others. We subvert
the claims of the powerful in the name of our servant
King. It was no mistake that the declaration group chose
to locate its statement on prayer under the section on
advocacy. We have no greater influence than when we
come before the God of the universe.

Armonia is a Christian agency working among the
poor of Mexico. Saul Cruz, who co-founded Armonia
with his wife, Pilar, teaches a course for development
professionals. On one occasion the course participants
questioned whether the work of Armonia could really
bring genuine change to the poor of Jalalpa. So the group
visited their urban transformation centre and Saul invited
them to talk to any of the children. They picked out a boy
who looked middle-class, thinking that he did not come
from the slum and that they had rumbled Saul's claims. It
was Daniel.

Saul and Pilar had met Daniel at the funeral of his
brother. They asked him back to the centre for a meal and
invited him to join in the centre's activities. They
confronted his mother and threatened her with legal
action if she did not stop demanding money from her
children. Daniel graduated from the centre's homework
clubs and was given an Armonia scholarship. With strong
loving discipline, Daniel has prospered and looks set to go
to university. In the context of a caring community, he has
become a Christian and participates in the centre's work
with younger children.

I met Daniel at the Armonia youth club. Over pizza – a
special treat – I asked the teenagers about their dreams.
One told me they hoped a generation touched by the work
of Armonia would bring change to the city through the
word of God. Another talked of the seed planted in them
driving out the darkness of Jalalpa. A third wanted to see
families change through their children. Their dreams

were not the dreams of many young people – dreams for success and prosperity. Instead, they hoped to bring change to their communities through the word of God. The challenge of integral mission is to share those dreams.

Introducing the Micah Network

Steve Bradbury

On 30 April 1999, in the Malaysian capital of Kuala Lumpur, a small international gathering of leaders of evangelical relief and development agencies commissioned a task group with the responsibility of developing a new international network.[3] The dream was that this new body would provide a framework in which the capacity and effectiveness of participating organizations would be enhanced, and at the same time develop a facility for collective action in key areas of mutual concern. The dream is now beginning to take shape.

From the beginning the task group was determined not to be midwife to yet another institution with its own internal demands, agenda and costly bureaucracy. Instead the focus was to be on creating self-funded events and processes that members could opt into and pay for according to their own needs and priorities. And so the Micah Network was created.

---

[3] The gathering was for the last General Assembly of the Interchurch Relief and Development Alliance, a WEF-related body established in 1980.

The choice of the name was not difficult – the prophet's words identify so clearly the imperative at the heart of our vision for the new network: 'What does the Lord require of you but to do justice, and to love kindness, and to walk humbly with your God?' (Mic. 6:8, NRSV).

The aim of the network was spelt out in the mission statement adopted by the Micah Network Co-ordinating Group – the renamed task group – at its first meeting in Kuala Lumpur in September 1999:

To create a dynamic process that facilitates collaborative action in:
• strengthening the capacity of participating agencies to make a biblically shaped response to the needs of the poor and oppressed
• speaking strongly and effectively regarding the nature of the mission of the church to proclaim and demonstrate the love of Christ to a world of need
• prophetically calling upon, and influencing, the leaders and decision-makers of societies to 'maintain the rights of the poor and oppressed [and] rescue the weak and needy' (Ps. 82:3–4).

The first Micah Network event, held in Thailand in October 2000, brought together 50 people representing 37 agencies to participate in an Asian regional workshop exploring principles and practices of Christian management and leadership. We were determined that the workshop would be strongly practical and participative. We expected that the collective experience and wisdom of those who came would provide an invaluable resource.

Our expectations were more than fulfilled. All those who participated were lavish in their praise – they deemed it time well spent. One wrote:

It was deeply stimulating and encouraging to meet together
with peer CEOs [Chief Executive Officers] and leaders of
international Christian relief and development agencies ...
We heard from leaders who shared about their lives and
organizations with openness, transparency and with vulnerability about what it means practically to be a Christian in
leadership. It was inspiring, affirming and challenging.

A second workshop on the same topic held in Addis
Ababa in May 2001 attracted 40 participants from nine
countries. Again, the evaluations indicated that the
content and process served very well the needs of those
who came.

The value and quality of the first major international
Micah Network event, the Oxford Consultation on
Integral Mission, can in part be gauged by the contents of
this book. The gathering in Oxford also made it clear that
the Micah Network is attracting the participation of a rich
diversity of individuals and organizations who together
represent an immense reservoir of experience and
insight.

I will always remember a conversation with a Ugandan
friend and pastor that took place a few years ago in
the small health clinic and AIDS counselling centre
constructed and resourced by his church to meet the needs
of a large sprawling Kampala slum. Thanks to Grace's
energy, skill and commitment the local church had
responded magnificently to the needs of the very poor
community to which they were a neighbour. A school had
been built and clean water supplied. Effective lobbying of
local government had succeeded in bringing about a
dramatic improvement in drainage and sanitation.

I asked Grace why he and his church had got so
involved in all this work. After all, it is not as though
'normal' parish responsibilities leave a lot of spare time.

His answer was brilliant. Apparently he had been in the parish for less than a year when he realized that a quarter of the babies he was baptizing were dying before they reached the age of six months. 'Steve', he said to me, 'I had to ask myself: What does it mean to be Christ's representative in this place?'

If the existence of the Micah Network somehow strengthens the work and witness of churches like Grace Kaiso's, and enables their experience and understanding to influence the theology and practice of the evangelical church world-wide, we will have achieved something of great importance. If, in addition, we are able to facilitate international co-operation that results in a more effective delivery of relief and development to poor communities, and if we are able to foster a similar co-operation that results in successful international advocacy for justice for poor communities, then the dream will well and truly become a reality. It is for this that we pray.

For more information on the Micah Network visit www.micahnetwork.org.

The *Micah Declaration* on Integral Mission

Preamble

The Micah Network is a coalition of evangelical churches and agencies from around the world committed to integral mission. Convened by this network, 140 leaders of Christian organizations involved with the poor from 50 countries met in Oxford in September 2001 to listen to God and each other for mutual learning, encouragement and strengthening as we serve the cause of the kingdom of God among the poor.

Our meeting coincided with the aftermath of the terrorist attack on the World Trade Centre in New York and the Pentagon in Washington DC. We express our abhorrence at this atrocity. God grieves for the more than 7,000 people who died and the many thousands who have been sadly affected. At the same time we recognize that many more thousands die unnecessarily each day, especially in the poor countries of the world, because of the evil alliance of injustice and apathy. God also grieves over these deaths. We want to call the attention of the church and the world to this daily outrage against human beings made in the image of the Creator.

We recognize too the symbolic meaning of this act of terrorism. In his day Jesus interpreted the butchery of Pilate against the Galileans as an opportunity to repent. Could it be that this act against the symbols of Western economic and military power is a call to repentance?

As we gathered, we heard of the devastating effects that globalization is having on poor communities around the world. We recognize the importance of the market for a healthy economy, but we reject giving the market ultimate status, allowing consumer goods to define personal identity and leaving the plight of the poor to market forces. We name this as idolatry. Although globalization is contributing to the creation of more open societies, on the whole it means the massive exclusion of the poor. Perhaps the most critical social task for the church in our generation is to offer a compelling alternative to the unjust imbalances in the world economic order and the values of its consumer culture. God is calling us to build global twin towers of justice and peace. We need to create a coalition of compassion.

During our time together, we have been deeply moved by the heart cry of those who suffer as well as by the astounding possibilities of change through Jesus' compassion. We have heard of the pain and blessing of accompanying people dying of AIDS in a town in Zimbabwe in which a third of the population have HIV. We heard of the life-changing experience of touching a limbless child in a Bosnian cellar and the story of a community kneeling together to confess their complicity in a culture of violence in Mexico. We were inspired by the transforming power of the gospel in the lives of drug addicts in Central Asia and advocacy on behalf of children forced into prostitution and bonded slavery.

Integral Mission

Integral mission or holistic transformation is the proclamation and demonstration of the gospel. It is not simply that evangelism and social involvement are to be done alongside each other. Rather, in integral mission our proclamation has social consequences as we call people to love and repentance in all areas of life. And our social involvement has evangelistic consequences as we bear witness to the transforming grace of Jesus Christ. If we ignore the world we betray the word of God which sends us out to serve the world. If we ignore the word of God we have nothing to bring to the world. Justice and justification by faith, worship and political action, the spiritual and the material, personal change and structural change belong together. As in the life of Jesus, being, doing and saying are at the heart of our integral task.

We call one another back to the centrality of Jesus Christ. His life of sacrificial service is the pattern for Christian discipleship. In his life and through his death Jesus modelled identification with the poor and inclusion of the other. On the cross God shows us how seriously he takes justice, reconciling both rich and poor to himself as he meets the demands of his justice. We serve by the power of the risen Lord through the Spirit as we journey with the poor, finding our hope in the subjection of all things under Christ and the final defeat of evil. We confess that all too often we have failed to live a life worthy of this gospel.

The grace of God is the heartbeat of integral mission. As recipients of undeserved love we are to show grace, generosity and inclusiveness. Grace redefines justice as not merely honouring a contract, but helping the disadvantaged.

Integral Mission with the Poor and Marginalized

The poor like everyone else bear the image of the Creator. They have knowledge, abilities and resources. Treating the poor with respect means enabling the poor to be the architects of change in their communities rather than imposing solutions upon them. Working with the poor involves building relationships that lead to mutual change.

We welcome welfare activities as important in serving with the poor. Welfare activities, however, must be extended to include movement towards values transformation, the empowerment of communities and co-operation in wider issues of justice. Because of its presence among the poor, the church is in a unique position to restore their God-given dignity by enabling them to produce their own resources and to create solidarity networks.

We object to any use of the word 'development' that implies some countries are civilized and developed while others are uncivilized and underdeveloped. This imposes a narrow and linear economic model of development and fails to recognize the need for transformation in so-called 'developed' countries. While we recognize the value of planning, organization, evaluation and other such tools, we believe they must be subservient to the process of building relationships, changing values and empowering the poor.

Work with the poor involves setbacks, opposition and suffering. But we have also been inspired and encouraged by stories of change. In the midst of hopelessness we have hope.

Integral Mission and the Church

God by his grace has given local churches the task of integral mission. The future of integral mission is in planting and enabling local churches to transform the communities of which they are part. Churches as caring and inclusive communities are at the heart of what it means to do integral mission. People are often attracted to the Christian community before they are attracted to the Christian message.

Our experience of walking with poor communities challenges our concept of what it means to be church. The church is not merely an institution or organization, but communities of Jesus that embody the values of the kingdom. The involvement of the poor in the life of the church is forcing us to find new ways of being church within the context of our cultures instead of being mere reflections of the values of one dominant culture or sub-culture. Our message has credibility to the extent that we adopt an incarnational approach. We confess that too often the church has pursued wealth, success, status and influence. But the kingdom of God has been given to the community that Jesus Christ called his little flock.

We do not want our church traditions to hinder working together for the sake of the kingdom. We need one another. The church can best address poverty by working with the poor and other stakeholders like civil society, government and the private sector with mutual respect and a recognition of the distinctive role of each partner. We offer the Micah Network as one opportunity for collaboration for the sake of the poor and the gospel.

Integral Mission and Advocacy

We confess that in a world of conflict and ethnic tension we have often failed to build bridges. We are called to work for reconciliation between ethnically divided communities, between rich and poor, between the oppressors and the oppressed.

We acknowledge the command to speak up for those who cannot speak for themselves, for the rights of all who are destitute in a world that has given 'money rights' greater priority than human rights. We recognize the need for advocacy both to address structural injustice and to rescue needy neighbours.

Globalization is often in reality the dominance of cultures that have the power to project their goods, technologies and images far beyond their borders. In the face of this, the church in its rich diversity has a unique role as a truly global community. We exhort Christians to network and co-operate to face together the challenges of globalization. The church needs a unified global voice to respond to the damages caused by it to both human beings and the environment. Our hope for the Micah Network is that it will foster a movement of resistance to a global system of exploitation.

We affirm that the struggle against injustice is spiritual. We commit ourselves to prayer, advocating on behalf of the poor not only before the rulers of this world, but also before the Judge of all nations.

Integral Mission and Lifestyle

Integral mission is the concern of every Christian. We want to see the poor through the eyes of Jesus who, as he looked on the crowds, had compassion on them because they were harassed and helpless like sheep without a shepherd.

There is a need for integral discipleship involving the responsible and sustainable use of the resources of God's creation and the transformation of the moral, intellectual, economic, cultural and political dimensions of our lives. For many of us this includes recovering a biblical sense of stewardship. The concept of Sabbath reminds us that there should be limits to our consumption. Wealthy Christians – both in the West and in the Two-Thirds World – must use their wealth in the service of others. We are committed to the liberation of the rich from slavery to money and power. The hope of treasure in heaven releases us from the tyranny of mammon.

Our prayer is that in our day and in our different contexts we may be able to do what the Lord requires of us: to act justly and to love mercy and to walk humbly with our God.

27 September 2001

Part One

Integral Mission

Integral Mission in the Teaching of Jesus: Matthew 20:1–16

Elaine Storkey

In Matthew 20:1–16 Jesus tells a parable to illustrate the kingdom of heaven. A vineyard owner hires labourers from early in the morning – probably around 6.00 am – right through the day. Every three hours or so he goes back to the marketplace and, finding people still with no work, hires more of them. The last group start work at 5.00 pm, so they work for just one hour. When pay time comes, the last are first to be paid and to everyone's amazement they receive a full day's pay. You can imagine what the ones who were hired first must have been thinking. They will be earning a small fortune, for they have worked ten times the hours of this final group. But in fact they receive the same as everyone else and so they complain. Like the elder son in the parable of the prodigal, they feel they have been cheated. But the vineyard owner says: 'No, this is right. This is what we agreed. I am giving you the full entitlement. I just want to be generous to the others.'

This is a strange picture of the kingdom of God. Whether we like the picture depends on who we are in the story. If you are successful, hard-working, diligent and strong – one of those who gets up early to work and labours all day – it does seem unfair. You bear the heat of the day and do not reap the reward you expect, given what others have got for virtually nothing. But if you are one of the poor, the marginalized, one whom no one has hired because the system somehow worked against you, this is a wonderful story. For those not normally included in the choices the powerful make, this picture of the kingdom is reassuring and thrilling. Suddenly they are no longer disadvantaged, but favoured; no longer treated with contempt, but with unexpected and overwhelming generosity.

This parable opens up three different, but interrelated, areas of meaning.

1. A Parable about Jew and Gentile

The Jews were chosen by God and called to live faithfully for him. They have been the bearers of God's name among the pagans. They have made sacrifices for God, kept the Law, repudiated evil, not squandered God's resources, honoured the land, not bowed the knee to Baal. They have always been secure in their identity as the people of God and in their knowledge of God's special blessings on their faithfulness. But in this story we see there is to be a change. They find themselves treated with no more privileges than the Gentiles who come so much later to faith in the one true God. The Gentiles, those with little to offer God and who have not struggled for righteousness, are to be accepted on equal terms. For the Jews, this hurts.

This parable anticipates the issues that will face the early church about inclusion and acceptance. It antici-pates Paul's quarrel with the Judaizers, who insist that the Gentiles must be brought under the Law before they can become Christians. Paul will insist that this is wrong for it undermines the salvation of Christ and the atoning work of the cross. Those who come last will be as acceptable to God as those who were first chosen. The basis of our acceptance before God is not our works, but his love.

2. A Parable about Works and Grace

This leads to the second meaning, that of works and law. The workers have different bases for how their work will be treated. The first group of workers are those who rely on the law. They have made a binding agreement and they will receive the just reward for their work. Their trust is in the contract. But those hired later have no contract. They are simply told by the vineyard owner that he will pay them what is right. But right in whose eyes? They are at the mercy of the employer. They can only trust in the mercy of the one whose service they have entered. But when pay time comes they find that trusting in the vineyard owner offers much greater security than any contract could ever offer, for, instead of mercy, they are given grace. They are not simply released from what they do deserve (in this case, little consideration); they are given what they do not deserve.

This issue of the grace of God is what separates the Christian faith from all other religions. This came home to me when I taking part in a broadcast discussion with an Islamic professor and a Jewish rabbi. We were discussing how one could tell a real believer from a counterfeit. Both contributors listed the things that a real believer would have to do to be recognized. The question was put to me: 'What would a Christian have to do?' I could only answer that a Christian has to do nothing. We only open empty hands to God to have them filled by his grace. This reply caused great consternation in the Muslim who reacted strongly and accused me of having a 'cosy' and easy view of God, and of undermining God's holiness. My reply was that Christianity did the opposite. We recognized that God is so holy that there was no possibility of meeting his standards. That was why we rely so entirely on the grace of God in Jesus Christ, who met God's requirements for us and reconciled us to God. This did not satisfy the Islamic professor at all, and he argued more vehemently until the rabbi put an arm across his shoulder and said, 'My dear friend, you will have to simply accept what she says. You and I will never understand this. But this "grace" is what Christianity is all about. It is what makes Christians so different from Jews or Muslims.' I was grateful that he had understood the heart of the Christian gospel.

Here in the parable there is grace and mercy based not on works or contract, but on the very nature of God. It is undeserved, but God gives it anyway.

3. A Parable about Justice and Compassion

But there is also a lesson in this parable about justice. There is no suggestion that those who get work early are in any sense wrong to do so. They are not out to harm others. They are good workers, keen to get the job done and to receive what is rightly theirs. What they receive comes by fair means and they are entitled to it. But these people are the strong ones. They are economically advantaged. They have learned to work the system. They have the self-confidence that is built up through the dignity of work and reaping its reward, and those doing the hiring always go for these people. They do not want to spend time and money teaching people new skills when they can get people who know the system already. Those who work hard for the rich often receive rewards, as they do in this parable. They have their contract and know their rights. They are used to operating in a rat race, where, as one writer once remarked, even if you win, you are still a rat.

But what about those in the story who are not hired? Having no work makes them economically weak. They have children to feed and would love to work. As the day wears on they become yet more vulnerable. By 5.00 pm they must be feeling desperate, willing to work for any price just to stay alive. They are what capitalist dreams are made of: people so poor they will take whatever is offered and say nothing.

But the vineyard owner does not exploit them. He does not treat them as commodities, using them for his own profit. He pays them the same as the strong and successful. He gives them back their self-respect and acknowledges their dignity.

Then, ironically, the successful complain that this is not fair! What Jesus spells out for us so clearly is that all too often the rich and successful do not want justice and compassion. They, and sometimes we, can resent generosity shown to the poor, for they want to keep their privileges and differentials. They want to stay at the top – it is the place they have earned.

Jesus shows us that we get what we earn. The workers all got their pay – it was a just and honourable transaction. The vineyard owner was no one's debtor. But what we cannot earn is the grace of God, for that is a free gift from God's heart of compassion. And it is grace that also redefines justice. Justice is not merely honouring a contract. It is also recognizing the bigger picture. It is looking at the way things conspire against the poor.

The message of this parable for the global church and for the governments of the world is that we need this bigger picture of justice. We need to understand the exclusions and vulnerabilities in our world. In our concern for just relationships between the peoples of the globe we might need to go the extra mile to care for the disadvantaged and honour the vulnerable.

The picture that the prophet Isaiah offers us of justice, where we spend ourselves on behalf of the poor and we break the yoke of oppression, is one that the vineyard owner puts into practice in his own backyard. It is the pattern that Jesus holds out for us all to follow, for this, he says, touches deep into the justice, mercy and grace of the loving heavenly Father. And this is what it is like in the kingdom of God.

Integral Mission in the Ministry of Jesus: Luke 7:36–50 and 19:1–10

Elaine Storkey

The two encounters with Jesus in Luke 7:36–50 and 19:1–10 might not seem on the surface to have much to do with integral mission, justice or indeed with each other. But on closer examination the issues are very pertinent. The two people, a man and a woman, are different. But they have some things in common. Neither of them suffers obvious financial hardship, but they are nevertheless marginalized people of Jewish culture. They are both despised by the upright; both rejected by the religious mainstream. And they both become the centre of issues of hospitality.

Luke 19:1–10

The story of Zacchaeus is one that we still like to tell to children. Yet its context and implications are anything but childlike. The context is the Roman occupation of Israel. The Jews are suffering not only the indignity of having their independence denied and their authority usurped;

they are also obliged to pay for the privilege. The burden of taxation is clearly heavy, and made much worse by the fact that the tax collectors are most often Jews themselves, who make a substantial livelihood by colluding with the occupiers. Zacchaeus is hated by his fellows. He is rich because he is paid well, but rich also because he is corrupt. He cheerfully takes his cut out of the pockets of those whose taxes he handles. And why not? The Romans are not going to worry unduly, and the whole system is unjust anyway. What does it matter if he cashes in and lines his pocket? It is adding only a little more to the exploitation and it brings him great rewards.

So it is not surprising that, when Zacchaeus joins the crowd to see Jesus passing by, no one bothers to let him through. Being short, he might have been shown courtesy if he had friends around. But instead he has to climb a tree to satisfy his curiosity. Not very dignified, we might think, but Zacchaeus seems, long since, to have let go of dignity or decorum. What follows is, of course, entirely unpredictable. Jesus, also unbothered about protocol, calls to Zacchaeus in the tree and invites himself to the tax collector's home.

Zacchaeus has rarely had the opportunity to offer hospitality. He is rich but has few friends: rich but impoverished relationally. So it is perhaps not surprising that Jesus takes the initiative here. He does not wait to be asked, for he is not going to be asked. Whatever the pleasures of Zacchaeus's wealth, they do little to bring him the confidence to invite someone home. What could possibly justify him in expecting others to receive hospitality from him?

Giving and receiving hospitality is close to the heart of Jewish society. Receiving hospitality is a mark of acceptance. And a true offer of hospitality is inevitably accompanied by vulnerability. It is not the natural domain of the rich. Henri Nouwen perceptively shows us the link between poverty and hospitality:

> It is the paradox of hospitality that poverty makes a good host. Poverty is the inner disposition that allows us to take away our defences and convert our enemies into friends. We can only perceive the stranger as an enemy as long as we have something to defend. But when we say, 'Please enter – my house is your house, my joy is your joy, my sadness is your sadness and my life is your life' we have nothing to defend since we have nothing to lose but all to give.[4]

I experienced something of this myself when visiting Mexico City and being received by the Armonia community. Although our hosts were indeed poor, we were overwhelmed by generosity. More than that, we were made to feel it was their privilege to receive us, to meet our needs of food and drink, and spend scarce resources on our behalf. We, who were rich, received from the poor and were grateful.

Here, Zacchaeus is asked to give to Jesus. He can hardly believe his ears. I imagine he must have almost fallen out of the tree. The text itself leaves us in no doubt that he hurried down to welcome Jesus.

Two responses

In the aftermath of Jesus' act of inviting himself, two things happen. The first is that the good, upstanding religious people begin to grumble. It is appalling that Jesus is about to go and 'be the guest of a sinner'. Is he not aware that this man is an extortioner who looted the poor on behalf of the hated Roman occupiers? The second is

---

[4] Henri JM Nouwen, *Reaching Out* (London: Fount, 1980), 103.

that Zacchaeus makes an immediate and totally uncharacteristic response: 'Half my possessions, Lord, I will give to
the poor; and if I have defrauded anyone of anything,
I will pay back four times as much' (NRSV).

If this were not said in public, with many of those he
had no doubt defrauded within earshot, we would find it
hard to believe he could mean it. But with so many
witnesses he clearly does not intend this to be an idle
promise. So what has brought about this extraordinary
and overwhelming response? It is that the very act of
acceptance from Jesus put him under conviction and
made him face his life, his past, his collusion with
injustice, his disregard for the poor and his part in the
whole corrupt system. And in one electric encounter he
gives it all up. In fact, this is to have permanent
consequences for Zacchaeus. His wealth will disappear as
he gives away half of all he owns and recompenses four
times over those he has swindled in his years of cheating.
The crowd must have been gasping as they worked out
the level of refund they might expect.

It is interesting that Zacchaeus's response turns
towards his responsibility for the poor. Jesus' move
towards him does not convict him for not having been to
the synagogue lately, or for failing to observe properly the
High Days and Holy Days. Zacchaeus is not showing
great remorse for the fact that he has not tithed his mint, or
recited the daily prayers. His mind goes immediately to
the heart of what is wrong: that he has shown injustice
towards the poor and has cheated his neighbours of what
was rightly theirs. It is these sins he must now remedy.

It is interesting too that Jesus does not rebuke
Zacchaeus. He offers no sermon about the law, no judge-
ment about attitudes, no condemnation for the past and
no warning about the future. Instead, his response strikes
at the very core of our evangelical hearts: 'Today salvation

has come to this house, because this man, too, is a son of Abraham. For the Son of Man came to seek and to save what was lost.' This extraordinary comment needs some examination. Why does Jesus refer to 'salvation'? Zacchaeus has made no confession of faith in the saving power of Christ. He has simply declared that he will give half of what he owns to the poor.

Some people pit Jesus against Paul, and argue that although Paul talks of free grace, Jesus implies we must work for our salvation. Here is an example: this man has earned salvation through his promise of recompense and his good deeds to come. This dichotomy, however, is totally unfounded. Redemption through works is certainly not what Jesus is suggesting. He is pointing to Zacchaeus's declaration as the truest indication of repentance and faith, for this kind of response speaks more loudly than any creed. Far more than a mere statement of belief, it is the sign of a changed heart, the sign of an encounter with God, which results in totally uncharacteristic action. To renounce easy cheating in an unjust system and declare a new love for the poor is a mark of true grace.

Luke 7:36–50

In this second story, hospitality occurs at the beginning, not at the end. Jesus has been invited to the home of a leading Pharisee to eat with his other guests. As would be normal at that time, the meal was eaten, probably in a courtyard, in full view of passers-by and of the local people, who would be interested in watching the great and the good. Barely is the meal underway when a woman bursts in. She may have been watching the proceedings up to this point, but now she rushes to the table where Jesus is reclining and begins to pay him very special attention. Weeping, she bathes his feet with her tears, strokes and kisses them, pours an expensive bottle of perfume over them, and lets down her hair to wipe them dry. There is consternation from the onlookers and the guests, who mutter among themselves, but this is probably nothing compared to the horror experienced by the host at the scandalous demonstration that is ruining his dinner party.

I confess to having some sympathy with Simon the Pharisee. And if we were to transpose this episode into a contemporary context, the incident would lose nothing of its outrage. If a local church leader, a leading pastor or a bishop were to be paid this kind of attention by a professional prostitute we might feel justified in wondering how he normally spent his time in the evening. Another challenge to Jesus' credentials certainly does not go unstated. Those at the table ask themselves – and probably each other – 'Wouldn't this man, if he were really a prophet, actually know what kind of woman this was?' The implication is clear. If Jesus were the kind of person he was made out to be, he would certainly not tolerate this kind of physical touching and sensual behaviour, and would have got rid of the woman immediately.

Jesus' reply is to tell a story: a story of the cancellation of debt. It would be a familiar one. The principle of the cancellation of debt would be one that people knew about. It was neither radical nor reckless in the way that many people think of it today. It was a principle deeply embedded in the Mosaic Law and in the economy of the people of Israel: a principle that people believed in even if they did not practise it with great enthusiasm. It is significant that Jesus uses an economic principle to highlight a spiritual one. For us, it is usually the other way round. The story he tells demonstrates how those who owe much have more to be grateful about than those who owe less when both their debts are cancelled. Those who are forgiven much love much, and those who are forgiven little love little. Of course, there is irony in the point, for some are forgiven little because they do not realize how much in debt they are and do not seek its cancellation.

The story has a sting in its tail, however. To show the extent of the woman's gratitude, Jesus compares her gesture of love and hospitality with that shown by his host. In every way it has greatly exceeded it. The host did not greet his guest with a kiss, did not offer him water for his feet, and did not provide a towel to dry them. In fact, the reception given to Jesus was exceedingly poor. But the woman gave her own tears, her kisses and even her hair to care for his needs. Consequently, she has demonstrated in all that she has done the quality of the forgiveness that lives in her heart. When debt is fully acknowledged and fully cancelled, love and gratitude are the overwhelming responses. To drive the point home, Jesus receives the woman's attentions in front of everyone and tells her that her sins are forgiven.

Interpreting the response

For me, one interesting question is why the woman reacted the way she did, for gratitude towards someone does not have to be expressed in such an overt and public manner. Three answers occur to me.

First, she may have been deliberately compensating for the lack of hospitality that Jesus received. As she watched the various welcomes to the table she would have noticed that he was not given the respect and honour that a guest might have expected. People were going through the motions of welcome and acceptance, but there was no heart there. She could well have detected in the disregard shown towards him an indication of their deep disrespect.

But second, she may well have recognized in Jesus something of her own situation, for, like her, he was some-one rejected. Like her, he was wanted for what he could bring others, sought for what he had and could give. Jesus was a novelty. He performed miracles. He attracted crowds. Having him at the table brought reflected status and honour, and this was what Simon enjoyed. In a similar way, the woman was used to being wanted for what she could give. She met people's sexual needs. She could give them pleasure. She was used to people taking her body and her sexuality, but for themselves. They wanted some-thing from her, but they did not want her. Here, she could see that Jesus was in the same position, and recognized in his humiliation her own story as both a commodity and an outcast. In her very act of weeping and kissing she owned the comparison and identified herself with him.

A third interpretation also offers itself. Like Zacchaeus, this woman was making a public renunciation of her own past, for she was bringing to Jesus her trade. She was doing what she might have done to so many men in order to arouse and stimulate them into sexual enjoyment. In touching Jesus, putting her flesh close to his flesh, kissing his feet and letting down her hair, she was using all her familiar services. Even the opening of the box of perfume could have had little ambiguity to the people round the table, for prostitutes always used perfume for the erotic arousal of their most valued clients. Yet this act was different. The woman was bringing all her past, her back-ground, her life, her brokenness, and leaving it with Jesus. It was not an erotic prelude to paid sex, but an unbridled act of the purity of love, of open hospitality. In one gesture, she was giving up to this man who had cancelled her debt: everything that had gone along with the life she once lived. His response was to accept what she brought, to receive her love for what it was, and to sing her praises before the self-righteous. More than any other reactions, these must have sent her out rejoicing into the future.

Summary

These two encounters with Jesus give us a deep insight into issues of mercy and justice. They tell us that people are not commodities, and yet that there are contexts where anyone can be used, demeaned and robbed of their self-respect. The people in these encounters are real people, and their reactions to Jesus are integrated reactions, not pious statements. They show, in ways that are utterly appropriate to them, what the welcome of Jesus means to them and the truth of their changed lives: justice to the poor; fair dealings with the weak; cancellation of debt; empathy with the rejected; love in action. In ways belonging intrinsically to their own stories, they bring the brokenness, pain, mistakes and sludge of past life and give them to Jesus. Here there is no hiding, no pretence and no whispering in the darkness. Instead, everything is revealed and shouted from the housetops as their lives encounter the power of love in the living God.

Jesus treats what they bring not with contempt but respect; not with rebuke but with joy; not with scorn but with warmth and acceptance. Here is safety and here is peace. Here, too, is justice and the kingdom of God.

Integral Mission and its Historical Development

C René Padilla

To what extent should the church be concerned for justice in society? Should Christians regard human rights as necessarily included within the sphere of their responsibility? If justice is a Christian concern, how can the church promote it in society? What are the biblical and theological criteria to evaluate the present-day global economic system? How can evangelical agencies best respond to the needs of the poor and oppressed in a globalized world? What are the priorities of international advocacy work from a biblically shaped perspective? How does action for justice relate to evangelism?

That we can raise these questions today throws into relief the changes that have taken place in the last few decades among a significant number of evangelicals around the world with regard to their understanding of the mission of the church. To be sure, the importance of integral mission is not unanimously accepted by evangelicals. Yet today many people who in the past dismissed such questions as irrelevant to mission are now open to a more holistic approach to mission.

The itinerary of the concept of integral mission can be traced by surveying the international evangelical conferences of the last few decades. A complete survey is not possible within this paper, but the attempt will be made to describe the process by which integral mission became a part of the evangelical agenda, beginning with the 1966 Wheaton Congress on the World Mission of the Church and concluding with the 1983 Wheaton Consultation on the Church in Response to Human Need.

From Wheaton 1966 to Chicago 1973

With almost 1,000 participants coming from 71 countries, the Congress on the World Mission of the Church (Wheaton, Illinois, 1966) was an important effort to rethink the mission of the church globally. The *Wheaton Declaration* was regarded by some as 'a thoroughly conservative statement from a conservative source'.[5] The *Wheaton Declaration* had, however, the virtue of recognizing that 'we are guilty of an unscriptural isolation from the world that too often keeps us from honestly facing and coping with its concerns'. It confessed the 'failure to apply scriptural principles to such problems as racism, war, population explosion, poverty, family disintegration, social revolution, and communism'. It urged 'all evangelicals to stand openly and firmly for racial equality, human freedom, and all forms of social justice throughout the world'.[6]

---

[5] Donald Gill, 'They Played It Safe in Wheaton', *World Vision Magazine* 10 (June 1966), 31.

[6] 'The Wheaton Declaration', *Evangelical Mission Quarterly* 2 (Summer 1966), 231–44.

Clearly, a new attitude with regard to the church's responsibility to the world was finding its way into evangelicalism. This new concern was related to the contribution of a number of participants from the Two-Thirds World. According to a conservative observer, 'their recommendations weighed heavily in determining the final shape of the Declaration'.[7] This helps to explain how such a document could come out of a mission conference held in the United States at a time when evangelicalism in that country was simply not interested in social change or social activism.[8]

The next important international meeting, the World Congress on Evangelism (Berlin, 1966), met under the motto 'One Race, One Gospel, One Task'.[9] Despite participants from 100 countries, the congress was 'predominantly Western in organization and expression'.[10] In his opening address Billy Graham reaffirmed his conviction that 'if the church went back to its main task of proclaiming the Gospel and people converted to Christ, it would have a far greater impact on the social, moral, and psychological needs of men than it could achieve through any other thing it could possibly do'.[11] He thus voiced a basic premise of the congress organizers and no advance was made towards a more comprehensive concept of mission. More significant were the follow-up regional congresses sponsored by the

---

[7] Harold Lindsell, *Christianity Today* 10 (29 April 1966), 795.

[8] Robert Fowler, *Christianity Today* 10 (7 January 1966), 338.

[9] The proceedings were published in Carl FH Henry and WS Mooneyham (eds), *One Race, One Gospel, One Task* (Minneapolis, Minnesota: World Wide, 1967).

[10] Arthur P Johnston, *The Battle for World Evangelism* (Wheaton, Illinois: Tyndale, 1978), 158.

[11] Billy Graham, 'Why the Berlin Congress', *Christianity Today* 11 (11 November 1966), 133.

Billy Graham Evangelistic Association. At all of them, with surprising regularity, speakers brought up the question of Christian social involvement as an issue intimately related to evangelism.[12]

A sensitive social conscience is an essential ingredient of integral mission, and a milestone in the awakening of the evangelical social conscience in the United States was the Thanksgiving Workshop on Evangelicals and Social Concern held in Chicago in 1973. The *Chicago Declaration of Evangelical Social Concern* was enthusiastically received by many people, who saw in it evidence that evangelicals were transcending the traditional dichotomy between evangelism and social responsibility.

Lausanne 1974

With all these antecedents, no one should have been surprised that the International Congress on World Evangelization (Lausanne, 1974) would turn out to be a definitive step in affirming integral mission as *the* mission of the church. In view of the deep mark that it left in the life and mission of the evangelical movement around the world, the Lausanne Congress may be regarded as the most important world-wide evangelical gathering of the twentieth century. It became a catalyst for evangelism and a matrix for theological reflection on issues that were placed on the evangelical missionary agenda by the *Lausanne Covenant*.

---

[12] See C René Padilla, 'How Evangelicals Endorsed Social Responsibility 1966–1983', *Transformation* 2:3 (1985); also published in C René Padilla and Chris Sugden (eds), *How Evangelicals Endorsed Social Responsibility* (Nottingham, UK: Grove, 1985).

On the relationship between the evangelistic and the societal dimensions of the Christian mission, paragraph 5 of the *Lausanne Covenant* stated:

> We affirm that God is both the Creator and Judge of all men. We therefore should share his concern for justice and reconciliation throughout human society and for the liberation of men from every kind of oppression. Because mankind is made in the image of God, every person, regardless of race, religion, colour, culture, class, sex or age, has an intrinsic dignity because of which he should be respected and served, not exploited. Here too we express penitence both for our neglect and for having sometimes regarded evangelism and social concern as mutually exclusive. Although reconciliation with man is not reconciliation with God, nor is social action evangelism, nor is political liberation salvation, nevertheless we affirm that evangelism and socio-political involvement are both part of our Christian duty. For both are expressions of our doctrines of God and man, our love for our neighbour and our obedience to Jesus Christ. The message of salvation implies also a message of judgment upon every form of alienation, oppression and discrimination, and we should not be afraid to denounce evil and injustice wherever they exist. When people receive Christ they are born again into his kingdom and must seek not only to exhibit but also to spread its righteousness in the midst of an unrighteous world. The salvation we claim should be transforming us in the totality of our personal and social responsibilities. Faith without works is dead.[13]

This is not merely an affirmation of the Christian duty towards social sin in terms of injustice, alienation, oppression and discrimination. It is also a rationale for

---

[13] See John Stott, *Making Christ Known: Historic Mission Documents from the Lausanne Movement, 1974–1989* (Carlisle, UK: Paternoster, 1996), 24.

Christian involvement in these social evils, beginning with the recognition of God as 'both the Creator and Judge of all men'. Christian social action is thus regarded as having a theological basis, as an expression of definite convictions with regard to God and humankind, salvation and the kingdom.

The importance of this statement coming out of a conference in which a high number of participants had all too often regarded evangelism and social concern as 'mutually exclusive' can hardly be exaggerated. The *Lausanne Covenant* not only expressed penitence for the neglect of social action, but it also acknowledged that socio-political involvement was, together with evangelism, an essential aspect of the Christian mission. In so doing it gave a death blow to attempts to reduce mission to the multiplication of Christians and churches through evangelism.

The following years, however, showed that, far from settling the matter, the Lausanne Congress had done little more than point to the need to deal with the role of social involvement for the sake of the integrity of the church and its mission. During the congress a large group had issued a document called *A Response to Lausanne* that aimed at highlighting issues of justice that had not been properly emphasized in the *Lausanne Covenant*. Its definition of the gospel of Jesus Christ as 'good news of liberation, of restoration, of wholeness and of salvation that is personal, social, global and cosmic' provided the strongest statement on integral mission formulated by evangelicals up to that date.

From Willowbank 1978 to Pattaya 1980

The *Lausanne Covenant* was received all over the world
with great interest and even exhilaration by Christians of
different theological persuasions. By contrast, others
interpreted Lausanne as a dangerous departure from
biblical truth and a tragic compromise with so-called
'ecumenical theology'. John Stott in particular came under
fire for defining social action as a 'partner of evangelism',
thus dethroning evangelism as 'the only historic aim of
mission'.[14]

In spite of its opponents, most of them identified with
the North American missionary establishment, integral
mission continued to find support among evangelicals,
especially in the Two-Thirds World. The issues it raised
became the motivating force for several world-wide
consultations that took place in the late 1970s and early
1980s, which explicitly dealt with, or at least touched on,
the question of justice. At the International Consultation
on Gospel and Culture (Willowbank, Bermuda, 1978), for
instance, it was recognized that 'too often we have
ignored people's fears and frustrations, their pains and
preoccupations, and their hunger, poverty, deprivation or
oppression, in fact their "felt needs", and have been too
slow to rejoice or to weep with them'.[15] The conference
underlined the need to take the incarnation of God in
Jesus Christ as a model for Christian witness. Even more
significant is a paragraph on 'power structures and

---

[14] Johnston, *The Battle for World Evangelism*, 292.

[15] Stott, *Making Christ Known*, 90. The proceedings were
published in John Stott and Robert T Coote (eds), *Gospel and
Culture* (Pasadena, California: William Carey, 1979) and *Down
to Earth: Studies in Christianity and Culture* (Grand Rapids,
Michigan: Eerdmans, 1981).

mission'. After referring to the poverty of the masses in the Two-Thirds World, it says 'their plight is due in part to an economic system which is controlled mostly by North Atlantic countries'.[16] In the face of this situation, the prophetic document calls for solidarity with the poor and the denunciation of injustice 'in the name of the Lord who is the God of justice as well as of justification'. It expressed concern about 'western-style syncretism' – 'perhaps the most insidious form of syncretism in the world today' – which is 'the attempt to mix a privatized gospel of personal forgiveness with a worldly (and even demonic) attitude to wealth and power'.[17]

The same concern for integral mission is reflected in other statements emerging from various conferences held in this period. The *Madras Declaration on Evangelical Social Action*, drafted at the All India Conference on Evangelical Social Action (1979), laid down the basis for responsible Christian action in the face of 'the increasing oppression of the underprivileged classes, the continuing entrenchment of casteism and the rising rate of communal violence'.[18] The *Pastoral Letter* issued by the Second Latin American Congress on Evangelism (Lima, Peru, 1979) echoed a deep concern for 'those who are hungry and thirsty for justice, those who are deprived of what they need in order to survive, marginalized ethnic groups, destroyed families, women who have no rights, young people dedicated to vice or pushed to violence, children suffering because of hunger, abandonment, ignorance, or exploitation'.[19]

---

[16] Stott, *Making Christ Known*, 101.

[17] Ibid., 102.

[18] The document is included in Chris Sugden, *Radical Discipleship* (London: Marshalls, 1981), 184–9.

[19] The letter was published with all the proceedings of the conference in *América Latina y La Evangelización en Los Años* 80 (México: FTL, 1980).

Of particular importance for the consideration of integral mission was the International Consultation on Simple Lifestyle (Hoddesdon, UK, 1980).[20] Despite its conciseness, the document issued at the end of the meeting, *An Evangelical Commitment to Simple Lifestyle*, turned out to be a significant statement of evangelical concern for justice.[21] The conference participants, 'disturbed by the injustices of the world, concerned for its victims, and moved to repentance' for their complicity in it, denounced environmental destruction, wastefulness and hoarding, and recognized their own involvement in them. They affirmed that involuntary poverty is 'an offence against the goodness of God', that 'God's call to rulers is to use power to defend the poor, not to exploit them', and that 'the church must stand with God and the poor against injustice, suffer with them, and call on rulers to fulfil their God-appointed role'. They committed themselves to re-examine their income and expenditure 'in order to manage on less and give away more' and 'to contribute more generously to human development projects'. Acknowledging, however, that changes in lifestyle without changes in the systems of injustice lack effectiveness, they claimed that 'servants of Christ must express his lordship in their political, social and economic commitments and their love for their neighbours by taking part in the political process'. Accordingly, they expressed their purpose to 'pray for peace and justice, as God commands' and to 'educate Christian people in the moral and political issues involved'. They said that 'all

---

[20] The proceedings and final document were published in Ronald J Sider (ed) *Lifestyle in the Eighties: An Evangelical Commitment to Simple Lifestyle* (Philadelphia: Westminster, 1982).

[21] Stott, *Making Christ Known*, 139–52.

Christians must participate in the active struggle to create a just and responsible society', including 'resistance to an unjust established order', and to be ready to suffer, for 'service always involves suffering'. JA Scherer is right in commenting that this conference touched on a number of 'themes seldom articulated with such passion in evangelical mission circles'.[22]

Clearly, as reflected in these documents, evangelicals had turned a corner at Lausanne with regard to their understanding of the social implications of the gospel and the mission of the church. It would not be difficult to prove, however, that the organizers of the next major international conference sponsored by the Lausanne Committee for World Evangelization (LCWE), the Consultation on World Evangelization (COWE, Pattaya, Thailand, 1980), made a special effort to ensure that the task of world evangelism was regarded as *the* mission of the church.[23] Under the motto 'How Shall They Hear?', Pattaya was to be 'a working consultation with the main objective of developing realistic evangelistic strategies to reach for Christ hitherto unreached peoples of the world'. That the organizers were almost exclusively concerned with the *how* of the (verbal) communication of the gospel was evident from the materials circulated in advance, which focused on 'people-groups' and 'homogeneous unit principle'. This preoccupation explains the tight control exercised by the leadership during the conference – there was the fear that discussion of the social aspect of

---

[22] Cited in David J Bosch, *Transforming Mission: Paradigms Shifts in Theology of Mission* (Maryknoll, New York: Orbis, 1991), 407.

[23] For a critique of COWE see Orlando E Costas, *Christ Outside the Gate: Mission Beyond Christendom* (Maryknoll, New York: Orbis, 1982), 135–61.

mission would divert attention from evangelism. In the words of one participant, 'Pattaya was somehow pre-packaged'.[24]

Much creative thinking, however, was done in the mini-consultations of the conference that met to consider the strategy to reach non-Christians in people-groups. As a result, the attempt to keep the conference within the straitjacket of a narrow definition of mission was counter-balanced at the grass-roots level. Some of the Lausanne Occasional Papers published after the Thailand consultation[25] demonstrate that several of the mini-consultations left aside the 'official' concern for strategy and 'went ahead on the gains of Lausanne'.[26] Some of the issues discussed in these groups became the basis for a *Statement of Concern on the Future of the Lausanne Committee for World Evangelization*, which, without the help of official publicity, was signed by 185 people within 24 hours.[27] This statement chided the Lausanne Committee for not being 'seriously concerned with the social, political and economic issues in many parts of the world that are a stumbling block to the proclamation of the gospel'. It called the Lausanne movement to help Christians 'to identify not only people-groups, but also the social, economic and political institutions that

---

[24] David J Bosch, 'In Search of Mission: Reflections on "Melbourne" and "Pattaya"', *Missionalia* 9 (April 1981), 17.

[25] See *Christian Witness to Marxists, Christian Witness to Large Cities* and *Christian Witness to the Urban Poor*, Lausanne Occasional Papers (Wheaton, Illinois: LCWE, 1980).

[26] Vinay Samuel and Chris Sugden, 'Let the Word Become Flesh', *Third Way* (September 1980).

[27] This document was included in Andrew Kirk, *A New World Coming: A Fresh Look at the Gospel for Today* (Basingstoke, UK: Morgan and Scott, 1983), 148–51.

determine their lives and the structures behind them that hinder evangelism' and to give guidance on how evangelicals lending support to repressive regimes or to unjust economic policies 'can be reached with the whole biblical gospel and be challenged to repent and work for justice'. This statement was presented to the LCWE as a 'genuine attempt to build bridges between evangelical Christians who at present are not yet agreed about the relationship between evangelization and socio-political involvement'. The conference leadership ignored it and no plenary discussion of it was allowed.

The *Thailand Statement*, adopted at the end of COWE, ratified Christian commitment to both evangelism and social action.[28] At the same time, however, it made clear that at least for the organizers of the consultation the time had come to reaffirm 'the primacy of evangelism'. Thus, under the influence of the American evangelical establishment, the statement made in the *Lausanne Covenant* that 'in the church's mission of sacrificial service evangelism is primary' was endorsed, even though it was also said that 'nothing contained in the Lausanne Covenant is beyond our concern, *so long as it is clearly related to world evangelization*' (emphasis added).[29] As Bosch rightly comments, 'the significance of this sentence lies in what it does *not* say – that nothing in [the] L[ausanne] C[ovenant] is beyond our concern, *so long as it clearly fosters Christian involvement in society*'.[30]

---

[28] Stott, *Making Christ Known*, 155–64.
[29] Ibid., 159.
[30] Bosch, *Transforming Mission*, 406.

From Grand Rapids 1982 to Wheaton 1983

In June 1982 the question of integral mission was taken up again at the International Consultation on the Relationship of Evangelism and Social Responsibility (CRESR) in Grand Rapids, Michigan.[31] The consultation defined the relationship between evangelism and social action in three ways. First, Christian social action is a *consequence* of evangelism, since those involved in it are Christians. In fact, they must be involved because they are saved 'for good works' and that means that social action is also one of the purposes of evangelism. Second, social action is a *bridge* to evangelism, since it expresses God's love and through that it eliminates prejudices and opens the way for the proclamation of the gospel. Third, social action is a *partner* of evangelism and is related to it in the Christian mission like two blades in a pair of scissors or the two wings of a bird.[32]

Of the primacy of evangelism the Grand Rapids document said that such primacy can only be affirmed in a limited, not in an absolute, sense. It considers that the primacy of evangelism is, in the first place, *logical*, since 'the very fact of Christian social responsibility presupposes socially responsible Christians, and it can only be by evangelism and discipling that they have become such'. Second, the primacy is *theological*, since 'evangelism relates to people's eternal destiny, and in bringing them good news of salvation, Christians are doing what nobody else can do'. But the Grand Rapids report also admits that the choice between evangelism and social action is 'largely conceptual' and that in

---

[31] The proceedings were published in Bruce Nichols, *In Word and Deed* (Grand Rapids, Michigan: Eerdmans, 1986).

[32] Stott, *Making Christ Known*, 182.

practice 'the two are inseparable' and 'they mutually support and strengthen each other in an upward spiral of increased concern for both'. If both evangelism and social action are so intimately related that their partnership is 'in reality, a marriage', it is obvious that the primacy of evangelism does not mean that evangelism should always and everywhere be considered more important than its partner. If that were the case, something would be wrong with the marriage!

Some critics feel that this consultation did not entirely succeed in avoiding a dualism between evangelism and social involvement.[33] According to them, by taking for granted that evangelism may be reduced to the *verbal proclamation* of the gospel, the Grand Rapids document laid the basis for a concept of mission as a marriage in which the two partners – word and action – are 'equal but separable'. A more biblical concept of mission suggests that there is no evangelism without a social dimension and there is no Christian social action without an evangelistic dimension. It must be noted, however, that the Grand Rapids document itself states that 'evangelism, even when it does not have a primarily social intention, nevertheless has a social dimension, while social responsibility, even when it does not have a primarily evangelistic intention, nevertheless has an evangelistic dimension'.[34] Such a statement can hardly be improved.

The strongest evangelical affirmation of commitment to integral mission in the last quarter of the twentieth century was the statement *Transformation: The Church in Response to Human Need*, which was drawn up at the end of the Consultation on the Church in Response to Human

[33] See Kirk, *A New World Coming*, 90–2 and Bosch, *Transforming Mission*, 406.

[34] Stott, *Making Christ Known*, 182.

Need (Wheaton, Illinois, 1983).[35] It recognizes that 'only by spreading the Gospel can the most basic need of human beings be met: to have fellowship with God'. But it is also critical of Christians who 'have tended to see the task of the church as merely picking up survivors from a shipwreck in a hostile sea'. It makes no allowance for any type of acquiescence in the face of social evil: 'either we challenge the evil structures of society or we support them'. It objects to 'many churches, mission societies, and Christian relief and development agencies [that] support the socio-economic *status quo*, and by silence give their tacit support'. It asserts that 'evil is not only in the human heart but also in social structures' and points to Jesus' example, who 'through his acts of mercy, teaching and lifestyle ... exposed the injustices in society and condemned the self-righteousness of its leaders'.

In the section dedicated to the local church, the Wheaton statement holds that congregations must not limit themselves to traditional ministries, but 'must also address issues of evil and social injustice in the local community and the wider society'. It calls upon aid agencies 'to see their role as one of facilitating the churches in the fulfilment of their mission' and warns them against the danger of exploiting the plight of the poor 'in order to meet donor needs and expectations'.

The final section is a strong affirmation of the coming of the kingdom of God in Jesus Christ as the basis for integral mission. 'We affirm', it states, 'that the Kingdom of God is both present and future, both societal and individual, both physical and spiritual ... It grows like a mustard seed, both judging and transforming the present age.' From this

---

[35] The proceedings of this consultation were published in Vinay Samuel and Chris Sugden, *The Church in Response to Human Need* (Oxford: Regnum, 1987).

perspective, eschatology is not an encouragement to escape into the distant future, but an incentive 'to infuse the world with hope, for both this age and the next'. 'As the community of the end time anticipating the End, we prepare for the ultimate by getting involved in the penultimate', and this means that we must 'evangelize, respond to immediate human needs, and press for social transformation'.

The Wheaton statement is quite an accomplishment as a synthesis of the theological basis for integral mission and a summary of the most significant questions that may be raised with regard to the church as God's agent for holistic transformation. It would be difficult to find in evangelical circles around the world any document drawn up after 1983 that would go further than the Wheaton statement in recovering an integral view of the church and its mission. The *Manila Manifesto*, issued by the Second International Congress on World Evangelization (Lausanne II), which took place in Manila in July 1989, did ratify in general terms the *Lausanne Covenant*, including the covenant's support of socio-political involvement.[36] But the lack of adequate attention to the question of justice during the congress was so clearly articulated by Valdir Steuernagel from Brazil in a ten-minute speech that he was allowed to give to the plenary at the very end of the congress.

In no way did the *Manila Manifesto* reach the level of the Wheaton statement in its affirmation of integral mission. In unequivocal terms the Wheaton statement affirmed social and political involvement as an essential aspect of the Christian mission. As Bosch has pointed out, 'For the first time in an official statement emanating from an

---

[36] See Affirmations Nos. 9 and 16 and Section Four of the Manila Manifesto in Stott, *Making Christ Known*, 227–49.

international evangelical conference the perennial
dichotomy [between evangelism and social involvement]
was overcome.'[37]

---

[37] Bosch, *Transforming Mission*, 407.

Integral Mission Today

C René Padilla

The progress of evangelicals towards an integrated approach to mission can be observed in the consultation and conference statements surveyed in the previous paper. Needless to say, it takes far more than good statements to enable Christians to make a meaningful contribution to integral mission. The statements, however, are indicative of a new mentality searching for change. One of the most positive results of this period was the articulation of theological concepts rooted in Scripture that provide a firm basis for integral mission.

A fine example of the theology of integral mission that evangelicalism has produced since the early 1980s are the statements of the Third and Fourth Latin American Congresses on Evangelism (CLADE III, 1992 and CLADE IV, 2000).[38] Both the *Quito Declaration* (1992) and the *Word, Spirit and Mission* statement (2000) leave no doubt that for a good number of evangelicals in Latin America integral

---

[38] The four CLADE documents (1969, 1979, 1992, and 2000) were published together in *Iglesia y Misión* 19.4 (December 2000).

mission is no longer a matter of debate but *the* way, according to the *Word, Spirit and Mission* statement:

> ... to participate in the mission of God by giving an integral witness to the gospel, by living an inclusive Christian spirituality, by carrying out a stewardship of creation which would put material reality at the service of the spiritual and use power for the well-being of others and for the glory of God, and by promoting reconciliation among races, social classes, sexes, generations, and the environment.

This advancing theoretical understanding of the Christian mission has resulted in the formation and strengthening of an amazing number of evangelical parachurch agencies committed to serving the poor. The Micah Network is a sign that thousands of Christians now recognize that the Great Commission is inseparable from the Great Commandment.

Without minimizing the importance of the large Christian service agencies characteristic of the wealthy world, it should also be recognized that much of the work in the front line is actually done by countless common believers. Among parachurch organizations there has been a paradigm shift towards a more kingdom-centred approach.[39] This shift, however, is not restricted to parachurch organizations. In the Two-Thirds World it extends to a myriad of local churches that are engaged in integral mission – not only *saying*, but also *being* and *doing* the witness to Jesus Christ.[40]

---

[39] Wesley K Willmer, J David Schmidt and Martyn Smith, *The Prospering Parachurch: Enlarging the Boundaries of God's Kingdom* (San Francisco: Jessey-Bass, 1998), xii.

[40] See Yamamori Tetsunao, Gregorio Rake and C René Padilla (eds), *Servir Con Los Pobres en América Latina* (Buenos Aires: Ediciones Kairós, 1997) and Darío López, *Pentecostalismo y Transformación Social* (Buenos Aires: Ediciones Kairós, 2000).

Another striking development in the last few decades has been the engagement of an increasing number of evangelical Christians in advocacy on behalf of the poor and oppressed. Paz y Esperanza (Peace and Hope) in Peru and the International Justice Mission in the United States are good illustrations of this development. Through them and similar institutions the call for involvement in questions of justice issued in the early eighties – especially at the Consultation on Simple Lifestyle (1980) and the Consultation on the Church in Response to Human Need (1983) – is being fulfilled.

At the same time, however, there are still many local churches and missionary societies that continue to reduce the Christian mission to 'saving souls'. A recent study of churches in Buenos Aires, Argentina, conducted by the Kairos Foundation, produced the following conclusions:

1. A predominant number of churches do not see themselves as part of the area in which they are located. They can ignore the city and the needs of people. Their efforts are centred on their self-preservation.
2. Only a few churches are really concerned for their respective neighbourhoods. Most do not listen to outsiders and are not interested in the real needs of people around them. Yet they regard themselves as saviours of the city because they do some good works for people.
3. It is rare to find churches that see themselves as part of, or partners with, their respective neighbourhoods, working with them in the solution of common problems, as incarnate in their communities.

This indicates that, while the cause of integral mission has made big strides in the last few decades, much more still needs to be done to help local churches see themselves as salt and light in concrete terms. For too long a narrow view of mission has been taken for granted. It is not surprising that the more holistic – and biblical – paradigm of mission should take time to be established.

Alongside this need for grass-roots change, much more needs to be done to respond to the growing gap between the rich and the poor around the world, characteristic of today's 'international economic order'. The 30 per cent of the world's population who live in Japan, Europe and the United States consume 80 per cent of the world's wealth. And in Brazil the top 20 per cent earn 32 times the income of the poorest 20 per cent.

One need not be an economics expert to realize that the so-called neo-liberal system is causing havoc around the world. Global capitalism is in deep crisis because it has placed money at the centre of life. The main beneficiaries of this system and the policies and procedures of the established order are the wealthy nations and the local oligarchic élites, but for the large majority of the world's population the result is poverty and misery.

Furthermore, the globalization of 'savage capitalism' is accompanied by the globalization of North American political and military interventionism for the sake of economic profit. The United States government in their official documents on their strategy for national security have made clear their intention to do all they can to protect 'the official security of our territory and that of our allies, and the security of our citizens *and our economic well-being*' (italics mine). 'We would even use', they say, 'our military power in a unilateral and decisive way, if necessary.'[41] More often than not the United States has lived up to this explicit policy of using violence to protect its economic interests. US military interventions – whether

---

[41] Cited in Luis Bilbao, 'Estados Unidos Alista un Ejército para el ALCA', *Le Monde Diplomatique* 3.27 (September 2001), 6.

directly or through surrogates – in countries like Panama, Guatemala, Cuba, Iran, Grenada, Dominican Republic and Nicaragua provide plenty of evidence to substantiate this claim. In 1989 Senator J William Fulbright, a former chair of the Senate Foreign Relations Committee, said: 'Since World War Two, the United States has become a globalist interventionist power.'[42] Senator Fulbright went on:

> It is understandably difficult ... to get off to a good start with a new revolutionary regime when you plot to kill its leaders. If we start to plan to assassinate leaders we don't like, as the CIA is believed to have done with Castro, you are only asking for trouble. It's self-defeating. It is against our interests. I don't think it ever succeeds. It gives others an excuse to engage in terrorism, to kill our ambassadors or citizens travelling abroad [or at home]. You start a process of terrorism that has far-reaching and unpredictable consequences. There is a good case to be made that we initiated it. We and some of our friends have initiated some of the worst aspects of modern terrorism.[43]

The recent brutal terrorist acts committed in New York and Washington on 11 September 2001 were abominable acts. But there should be no surprise if a country that sows violence for the sake of economic profit reaps violence. Unfortunately the recent terrorist blow has prepared the scene for a new military build-up and the resulting expansion of an economy heavily dependent on militarization. After all, militarization is a highly profitable business.

---

[42] J William Fulbright with Seth P Tillman, *The Price of Empire* (New York: Pantheon, 1989), 153.

[43] Ibid., 172.

Given these circumstances, the plight of the poor will change without a concerted effort on the part of people in wealthy countries. Perhaps the greatest challenge for Christians in the West with regard to world poverty is to rediscover their prophetic role at the centre of political and economic structures. As Lesslie Newbigin has put it:

> The ideology of the free market has proved itself more powerful than Marxism. It is, of course, not just a way of arranging economic affairs. It has deep roots in the human soul. It can be met and mastered at the level of religious faith, for it is a form of idolatry. The churches have hardly begun to recognize that this is probably their most urgent task during the coming century.[44]

The idolatrous shape of the contemporary economic system suggests that the time has come for evangelical service agencies to make educating Christians in the West to fulfil their prophetic task a priority. Much of the work of Christian service agencies is still focused on 'development'. Too often the assumption is that the rich countries are called to provide social models for the rest of the world; that they represent a higher stage of development towards which all other societies should evolve. In a world where injustice has become institutionalized on a global scale, however, Christians are called to bear witness to the God of love over and against the idolatrous materialism of our day as we wait for the fulfilment of God's promise of a new heaven and a new earth where justice will be at home.

---

[44] Lesslie Newbigin, *The Open Secret: An Introduction to the Theology of Mission*, (Grand Rapids, Michigan: Eerdmans, 1995), 95.

Integral Mission in Context

Tom and Christine Sine

Introduction:
Taking the Globalized Future Seriously

In the conclusion of his definitive work on the history of missiology, *Transforming Mission*, David Bosch states: 'The mission of the church needs to be constantly renewed and re-conceived.'[45] One of the major reasons for this constant renewal is that the context in which we live our lives, operate our churches and do mission keeps changing. In this paper we attempt to sketch some of the new challenges and opportunities we believe are facing the church in mission as we race into a new century.

We have found that very few churches or Christian mission organizations make any effort to make sense of how the context in which they are doing mission is likely to change before they plan. There is a tendency to plan as though the future is simply an extension of the present.

---

[45] Bosch, *Transforming Mission*, 519.

Futurists seek to identify driving forces for change. There is a widespread consensus that one of the major driving forces for change as we race into the twenty-first century is globalization. It is our belief that globalization is already changing the world in which we live, seek to serve Christ and think about mission. We join others and use 'McWorld' as a metaphor to characterize the globalization of our planetary society.

In the 1990s the global community moved into a new neighbourhood, which is discussed constantly in the business community, but seldom in the church. Overnight we moved into a new one-world economic order. Two major events directly contributed to this process of rapid globalization.

First, in the 1980s and 1990s we began hardwiring our planet at incredible speed into a single global electronic nervous system of satellites, fax machines and Internet communications. Borders are melting. Distance is dying. One and a half trillion dollars circulate through this global electronic nervous system every day, directly contributing to the rapid creation of this new one-world economic order.

Second, with the sudden end of the cold war all the centrally planned economies were thrown into the trash bin and for the first time in history virtually all nations in the world joined the free market race to the top. We have moved into a new neighbourhood that we have never lived in before: a one-world economic order. Even though this new boom economy has slowed and some fear a global recession, others are hopeful the economy will take on new life. Time will tell.

In spite of the protests at recent G8 conferences, there are many upsides to this new global economy. It is creating jobs and increasing wealth for a number of people in many different countries. The Internet has become an avenue for increasing international understanding and creating new forms of advocacy for justice, peacemaking and the care of creation. This new global economy has become in itself a tremendous force for promoting global stability for the simple reason that doing war gets in the way of doing business.

Globalization and the Future of the Poor

In the 1990s we saw an unprecedented explosion of wealth among the top 20 per cent of the world's population with the creation of more millionaires and billionaires than during any decade in history. The bottom 20 per cent of the world's population, however, have actually lost ground in this very competitive race to the top. The United Nations Development Programme states that 30 years ago the poorest 20 per cent of the world's population earned 2.3 per cent of the world's income. Now they earn only 1.4 per cent and that amount is still declining. At the same time the richest 20 per cent increased their share of global income from 70 per cent to 80 per cent.[46] Robert Wade, a professor of political economy at the London School of Economics, cited two very recent studies to express his concern regarding the apparent growing inequity. 'Between 1988 and 1993 ... the share of the world's income going to the poorest 10 percent of the world's population fell by over a quarter, whereas the share of the richest 10 percent rose by 8 percent.'[47]

One of the cardinal doctrines of this new global economy is that if we are allowed to buy one another's

---

[46] 'A Global Poverty Trap', *The Economist* (2 July 1996), 34.
[47] Robert Wade, 'Winners and Losers', *The Economist* (28 April 2001), 72–4.

banks and phone companies and fish in one another's ponds, it will automatically raise all boats. The following example from Uganda would seem to call this assumption into question. A European fish company contracted with the Ugandan government to build a large fish factory on the edge of Lake Victoria sends 200 tons of flash-frozen fish a week back to Europe. Of course there are some economic benefits for a few of the élite in Uganda, but tens of thousands of Ugandans can no longer afford to buy fish from their own lake because the European fish factory has driven up prices fourfold.

Even though global population growth is slowing, it will still grow from 6.2 billion today to between 8 and 10 billion by 2050. Most of that growth will be among our poorest neighbours in densely congested urban areas. Today almost half of the global poor are under 15. According to Bread for the World this growing economic disparity is likely to be dramatically increased in the next 25 years, when the huge population of children and young people in poorer countries hit the labour market. We will need to create two billion new jobs to respond to this challenge.[48]

One other trend should concern us. In this competitive race to the top a number of Western countries are trying to find ways to reduce the drag on their economies by cutting back spending in foreign aid and social programmes at home. This means that the church and private sector will increasingly be asked to address the growing physical needs of those left behind in this new global economy. The new United States Republican administration is already expressing hope that faith-based groups will play a greater role in responding to the needs of the poor overseas and at home.

---

[48] 'Hunger in a Global Economy' (Bread for the World Institute, 1998), 25.

Mission organizations involved in relief and development work and even church planting are going to need to increase dramatically their investment in vocational education for both young women and men, job creation and micro-enterprise development. Leaders in global missions will also need to explore how to respond to the new justice and environmental challenges that are a part of our new global economy.

Globalization and the Future of the Middle Class

Everywhere we work in Britain, Australia, New Zealand, Canada and the United States people tell us they are working harder and longer to stay even in this increasingly competitive global economy. In 1977 less than half of families in the United States relied on dual incomes. Today that figure has dramatically increased to two-thirds and is still climbing. Some women are working simply to help pay the bills and keep their heads above water. Others are working in order to buy extras. Similar trends are observable in other Western countries. In fact, a growing number of people in this new 24-hour, 7-day-a-week on-line economy work almost continually.

'McWorld' wants more, not only of our time, but also of our money. This new boom economy is not only an assets-based economy, but a shareholder economy. And shareholders do not want a 3 per cent to 5 per cent return on their investment. They want a 15 per cent to 30 per cent return if they can get it. The only way that can happen is for all of us to be persuaded to consume at levels never seen before on this planet so that yesterday's luxuries become today's necessities.

As a part of the need to keep the boom economy booming our young face escalating pressure to increase their consumption. Naomi Klein, in her book *No Logo*, documents how the marketers target the young much more directly, persuading them to try to find meaning, purpose and identity in the things they buy and the brands they wear. In other words they are moving into religion's domain.[49]

These trends mean that Christians in many of our Western countries have less time for family, prayer, Scripture, church or to volunteer for mission activities at home or abroad. This means that mission organizations need to increase significantly their investment to help their constituents find ways to steward their time more effectively if they want to have their continued involvement.

Some argue that if the pressure on us and our young to consume more continues it may be good for the global economy. But it will not be good for our humanity and spirituality or for the character of the church or for global mission. It will probably mean that many middle-class supporters of mission are likely to spend more on comfortable lifestyles and have less money left over to invest in word and deed mission.

Globalization and the Future of the Church

The good news is that the church in Africa, Latin America and parts of Asia is enjoying rapid growth. In the West there is a growing hunger for spirituality, particularly among the postmodern young. But there seems to be little interest in what most evangelical churches are offering. God, however, started raising up new youth churches in

---

[49] Naomi Klein, *No Logo* (New York: Picador Press, 2000).

the UK in the late 1980s. These are engaging the young far more successfully. We see a similar emergence of youth churches in Australia, New Zealand, Canada and the United States. They represent our best possibility in the West of reaching the postmodern young.

All our churches are going to be challenged to address not only the mounting physical needs that are filling our planet, but the growing spiritual needs as well. What is not generally recognized is that we are actually going backwards, not forwards, in world evangelization. Peter Brierley of Christian Research reports that 28 per cent of the world's people identify themselves as some brand of Christian: Protestant, Catholic or Orthodox. Because population growth is outstripping our best efforts at mission that percentage will decline to 27 per cent in 2010 and continue to decline after that.[50]

We are witnessing a new competitor for the hearts and minds of a new generation. In the past ten years we have seen the creation of a new borderless global youth culture. The marketers of 'McWorld' are not just selling products to the global young. They are consciously at work seeking to persuade the young to change their values so they will all buy the same products.

While there is a growing hunger for spirituality in the West, church attendance statistics in continental Europe are in free fall as it rapidly moves towards becoming a post-Christian culture. Church attendance in Britain fell from 10.2 per cent in 1980 to just below 8 per cent in the year 2000. In Australia weekly attendance is closer to 10 per cent but declining. Research in New Zealand suggests attendance is a little higher at 17 per cent, but in decline. In Canada the falling attendance rate is closer to 20 per cent,

---

[50] Peter Brierley, *Future Church: A Global Analysis of the Christian Community to the Year 2010* (London: Monarch, 1998), 33.

while Kirk Hadaway places church attendance in the United States at 24 per cent.[51]

The missing generation in the church in Europe, Australia, New Zealand, Canada and the United States is the under 35s. The young are disappearing from our churches in alarming numbers. In his seminars George Barna says that the 'buster' generation – those born between 1965 and 1983 – is the first generation in America that is not starting life with some kind of clear Christian heritage. The 'buster' generation in the United States attends church significantly less than any other generation.[52]

If the Western church is to have a future we need to target strategically the evangelization of the under 35s. We must also give the Christian young who are with the church greater responsibility for leading and reinventing the church for the twenty-first century, as young leaders are already doing in Britain. Between 2010 and 2030 the 'boomer' generation – those born between 1946 and 1964 – will retire, which will mean a serious decline in income to the Western church. Finally, since the 'buster' generation will be less numerous in our churches, have more college debt and spend a greater share of their income on housing, they will not be able to sustain the present level of giving to mission. Therefore, our reluctant forecast is, given current trends, that mission support from the Western church could go into decline by 2020 for the first time since the end of World War II. Declining resources would likely mean growing competition between word and deed missions.

---

[51] Tom Sine, *Mustard Seed Versus McWorld: Reinventing Life and Faith for the Future* (Grand Rapids, Michigan: Baker, 1999), 127–40.

[52] Barna Research Group, 'Church Attendance by Generation' (8 July 1998).

Alongside these demographic changes, in the United States an integrated approach to mission has been losing ground in recent years. The majority of American pastors have not heard of the *Lausanne Covenant*, let alone any of the follow-up consultations on an integrated approach to mission. As well as this there is a heated debate among evangelical leaders in the United States who are very much aware of the ongoing international conversation on integral mission. This debate was sparked by James Engle and Bill Dyrness's book *Changing the Mind of Missions: Where have we Gone Wrong?*[53] David Hesselgrave, Professor of Mission at Trinity Evangelical Divinity School, Deerfield, Illinois, expressed concern about the evangelical movement's slide into holistic mission and criticized the book for not supporting 'the priority of evangelism, reaching the unreached, and planting New Testament churches. Both the words "evangelical" and "mission" are thereby eroded.'[54] Furthermore, a number of evangelicals in the United States have embraced a view of social responsibility shaped largely by the religious right and the political right that largely ignores social justice issues.

René Padilla offers a definition of integration between word and deed mission in his book *Mission Between the Times*. He writes:

Both evangelism and social responsibility can be under-stood only in light of the fact that in Jesus Christ the kingdom of God has invaded history and is both a present

---

[53] James F Engel and William A Dyrness, *Changing the Mind of Missions: Where have we Gone Wrong?* (Downers Grove, Illinois: InterVarsity Press, 2000).

[54] David J Hesselgrave, 'Reform not Revolution', *Evangelical Missions Quarterly* 37.1 (January 2001), 92–3.

reality and a future hope … it is God's redemptive power
released in history, bringing good news to the poor, freedom
to the prisoners, sight to the blind and liberation to the
oppressed.[55]

We believe the kingdom of God is not only the key to an
integrated view of mission, but also offers a compelling
alternative to the aspirations and values of the global
consumer culture for our lives and communities of faith.

There is a growing discussion on the impact of
postmodernity. In the academy the issue is how we do
intellectual inquiry. But postmodernity is also stirring a
conversation in the church on how we think about faith
and even how we do mission. As a consequence there is
a growing movement away from the propositional
theology that has been an integral part of the evangelistic
message of most Western mission organizations involved
in church planting and evangelism.

As we struggle to define the relationship between
evangelism and social responsibility we will need to
rethink essential questions. What is the message of the
gospel of Jesus Christ and to what extent has it been
modified by our seeking to accommodate the rationalism
of modern culture? How do we communicate that
message in a postmodern world? What does it mean to
become a believer in a postmodern culture? Is it possible
to measure our mission results? How do we relate the
faith claims of the gospel of Christ to other religions in a
world of increasing religious pluralism?

---

[55] C René Padilla, *Mission Between the Times: Essays on the Kingdom* (Grand Rapids, Michigan: Eerdmans, 1985), 197.

Globalization and the Future of the Economy

While the influence of postmodernity is growing, modernity's influence also continues to grow. The creation of this new global economy is actually accelerating the rate at which the influence of modernity and Westernization is reaching into every corner of the planet. There seems to be little recognition of the threat modernity presents to the church. Evangelicals of course relentlessly do battle with modern culture on moral issues such as pornography on the Internet – and we should. But too often we treat the other messages of modernity – such as individualism, materialism and consumerism – as though they are value-neutral. Many evangelicals, for example particularly in the United States, tend to treat the free market, which is a product of modernity, as though it is simply a value-free economic mechanism that produces only positive outcomes.

Rob van Drimmelen, in an important book entitled *Faith in the Global Economy*, calls for the demystification of economics. He persuasively points out that the assumptions on which modern economics are based are far from being value-free.[56] At core, modernity and free market capitalism are driven by a vision of the better future – the so-called 'western dream' – that is inherently a different vision for the human future than that of the kingdom of God. How can Christians possibly hope to contend with the messages from modernity and our new global economy and keep in sight what is important if we have already unconsciously bought into the same dream for the better future that drives economic globalization?

---

[56] Rob van Drimmelen, *Faith in the Global Economy: A Primer for Christians* (Geneva: WCC, 1986), 1–6.

The *Oxford Declaration on Christian Faith and Economics* sounded a warning that we want to echo. 'There is ... the danger that the model of the market, which may work well in economic transactions, will be assumed to be relevant to other areas of life, and people may consequently believe that what the market encourages is therefore best or true'.[57] The growing message we hear from this new economic order is that the ultimate is defined in largely economic terms.

For decades, while talking about the importance of integral mission, we believe we have unwittingly exported a compartmentalized rather than integrated approach to discipleship all over the world. For example, we see middle-class Christians who increasingly derive their sense of life purpose, identity and meaning from where they work and what they buy. We see Christians at the margins, who, when they secure a good job, leave their poor communities behind and move into more affluent neighbourhoods where they can give their children the 'benefits'. Before we can answer the question 'what is an integral approach to mission?' we must answer first the question 'what is an integral approach to discipleship in our new global culture?'

In his book *The Integrity of Mission* Orlando Costas offers a prayer that still has not been fully answered. We need not only to join in this prayer for an integrity of mission, but to commit ourselves to see it become much more of a reality.

The true test of mission is not whether we proclaim, make disciples or engage in social, economic and political liberation, but whether we are capable of integrating all

---

[57] 'Oxford Declaration on Christian Faith and Economics', *Transformation* 7:2 (April 1990), 1–9

three in a comprehensive, dynamic and consistent witness. We need to pray that the Lord will liberate us not only from this stagnant situation, but he may liberate us for wholeness and integrity in mission.[58]

---

[58] Orlando E Costas, *The Integrity of Mission* (San Francisco: Harper & Row, 1979), 75.

Case Study

Networking for Integral Mission: El Camino Network, Latin America

Robert Guerrero

Overview

Organization
El Camino Network, Latin America

Project description
A network of Latin American organizations and churches
committed to integral mission

Issues
Networking, mobilizing the church, integral mission

Context

El Camino Network for Integral Mission in Latin America represents a coming together of many church and ministry leaders seeking a common road for our churches in Latin America. During the Fourth Latin American Congress on Evangelism in Quito, Ecuador (CLADE IV, 2000), the Consultation on Integral Mission and Poverty united over 300 pastors and leaders from throughout the continent to reflect on the reality of Latin America from a sociological and theological perspective. The primary emphasis that came out of the consultation discussion was the cry of the moment – 'what can the local church *do* to respond to the urgent needs of our communities in Latin America?' The search for a practical answer to this question is what gave birth to La Red Del Camino – 'The Network on the Way for Integral Mission in Latin America'.

El Camino Network seeks to respond not only to a continent burdened by economic injustice, but to a culture with elements that perpetuate poverty at many levels. Our political and cultural heritage is plagued by our colonial history, the effects of which are still experienced today. Totalitarian governments have been replaced by semi- or pseudo-democracies that have only served to perpetuate dependency and underdevelopment. The few that benefit from these systems serve as hinges for north–south policies at the expense of many. Today's global-ization and neo-liberal agendas are accelerating the process under the umbrella of 'progress', making us increasingly more dependant on the north and the economic power brokers. These apparent advances have lead to chaotic and unplanned urbanization – breeding grounds where crime, unemployment, underemployment, domestic violence and other social maladies abound.

The predominant cultural mindset in Latin America is Roman Catholic. Although the evangelical expression of the Christian faith has shown significant growth in the last decades, our continent is still culturally Catholic. The evangelical expression of the church, for example, tends to be more mystical, spontaneous or ritualistic than its Protestant counterpart to the north in its practice of the faith. Thus the focus is an escapist individualism rather than a responsible community of the kingdom. Although there are both Catholic and evangelical responses to the various needs of our continent, they are not representative of the majority among the communities of faith. These elements have tended to ferment a more individualistic and dualistic form of religion that at best ignores, and at worst perpetuates, the social evils that permeate our Latin American context.

Description

El Camino Network's vision is to 'prepare the way for the manifestation of the glory of God in terms of love and justice in the Latin American society through the local church'. Our mission is to 'accompany local churches in their development as communities of God's kingdom and transformational agents in their respective contexts'. Essentially, our purpose is to walk with the local church in the implementation of its integral and transformational mission.

El Camino Network is in its early stages, but we already express this purpose through the work and experiences of our members. Most of the member ministries are connected to at least one local or regional network that is committed to local church-based integral ministries. As these local and regional efforts come together we join forces to advance the cause throughout the continent. The following five action areas and their associated objectives are the result of our first network session (January 2001).

a. *Investigation and organization*

- identify and promote the documentation of experiences throughout Latin America in local church-based holism and development
- encourage the study of the Latin American contextual realities that affect the life and mission of the local churches
- stimulate biblical theological research and reflection on the integral mission of the church
- identify available resources for integral mission

b. *Relations*

- promote fellowship among the members of the network, local churches and other networks and pro-ecclesiastical entities at a local, regional and international level
- stimulate co-operation and co-ordination among local churches, communities and institutions towards the advancement of the integral mission

c. *Formation*

- facilitate the development of a contextual biblical theology towards a more integral ecclesiology
- promote a spirituality that takes into account the totality of the human life
- promote a model of leadership that incarnates and promotes integral mission

- deepen the commitment to the integral mission through liturgy
- facilitate the institutional strengthening of the practitioners of the integral mission

d. Resources

- stimulate the sharing of information, and technical and financial resources among the Christian community at large and the members of El Camino Network in particular

e. Communication

- share the vision, concepts and principles of integral mission
- broadly communicate the vision, mission, objectives and experiences of the network

Outcomes

Our success will be measured in the practical expression of integral mission at the local church level throughout our continent. The fellowship among our members will result in a unification of resources towards the advancement of the cause. Dominican Republic is an example of the implementation of several of the objectives stated previously.

The Network of Churches and Ministries for Integral Mission in Dominican Republic is represented in El Camino Network by two of its members. What began as a casual meeting between a few members of diverse ministries (Youth for Christ, World Vision, ASPIRE, Esperanza Foundation, Intercambio, Iglesia Comunitaria

Cristiana, Comunidad Cristiana International and others) has turned into a national network that has a discipleship role towards many local churches around the country. What united these groups was a passion to see local churches serving holistically in their communities. The first national conference on holistic mission was celebrated in 1999 with over 40 pastors and leaders. In 2001 the Dominican Republic network gathered over 100 leaders for the third annual conference. All who participated are committed to an holistic model of ministry. Each of these participating churches and ministries is in fellowship with at least one, sometimes several, of the members of the national network. Some even operate as regional and local networks themselves. Through the network we provide training, theological formation, model ministries, the sharing of logistical and human resources, educational materials and local workshops. Workshops offered at the last conference included:

- transitioning from a traditional model to a prevailing model of ministry
- becoming a contagious Christian
- the church's prophetic role in proclamation, social action and liturgy
- church projects for community transformation
- the church as a community of believers
- the church as a community of hope towards outsiders
- preparing messages that are sensitive to unbelievers
- diagnosing the needs and realities of your community
- resource development for integral mission
- integrated models of discipleship

The purpose of these encounters is to expand the vision and equip leaders of local churches who already practise holistic ministry in their communities. As we identify and train these leaders our goal is to provide visible and working expressions of church-based holistic ministry. These churches serve as models for others who become interested in doing the same. Our growth model is more through attraction, strategic accompaniment and relationships than through open-ended invitations. As local churches become active practitioners of the mission they join the network with the commitment to serve in the advancement of the cause for the development of integral churches. In this manner we ensure that the network is both practical and reflexive in nature.

Impact

The results have been amazing given the short history of the network and the informal structure under which it operates. In one marginalized neighbourhood, for example, four churches and a pro-church ministry called Living Waters have united to build a community youth centre. One of the main problems in the community is the violence and delinquency among young people who are unschooled and jobless. The youth centre hopes to reach these young people through sports ministry, vocational training, literacy programmes, tutoring and spiritual formation. Through this collaborative effort, the churches and the Christian NGO are creating a kind environment for this community. It is like an oasis in the desert. The centre is yet to be completed and, while under construction, it has been used by the local churches to hold workshops on marriage enrichment and family issues. Eventually, the local churches hope to provide additional services to the community through the centre, such as a community library, information centre, basic medical and dental attention and childcare for young mothers. All of the pastors from the local churches involved have

Case Study   85

participated in the network conferences on holistic
ministry.

Another example flows from the experience of Pastor
Francisco Sanchez Roso and the local Assemblies of God
church of the small rural community of Peralta. Francisco
has internalized the vision of an holistic church, bringing
hope and life to the community. As a local church they
have participated in a community health programme
and created a community centre. The centre is formally
recognized as a vocational training centre of INFOTEP, the
governmental vocational training agency. It also serves as
a gathering place for the young people of the community
for music, education and recreational activities. The
involvement of the church in the life of the community
and their collaboration with civic, communal and
religious organizations for local development efforts has
made them a respected voice in Peralta, and the church is
growing as a result, so much so that earlier this year the
church participated in a call to develop a community
health programme funded by the Inter-American
Development Bank. The local church was chosen to be the
implementing organization for this internationally
funded, community-wide health programme.

All these local efforts have opened the door for local
churches to be accepted in the community. Iglesia
Comunitaria Cristiana (ICC), for example, has been
serving in the city of Santo Domingo for six years. This
traditionally Catholic community was once labelled 'the
burial ground of evangelical pastors'. In the previous 15
years efforts to plant an evangelical church within its
borders had failed. Currently ICC has a community centre
hosting hundreds of people daily through its various
ministries. The after-school programme serves more
than 80 children from very low-income families. The
community gym has an active membership of over 500.

The centre is also home to a seamstress school and a music academy. In addition ICC works with addicts in their recovery process. Although ICC is the youngest church in the community, it is the most readily recognized by the community at large, and the most attended. More than a third of its membership is involved in its diverse ministries. Its enterprises generate income, serve the community and witness to the gospel – all at the same time. ICC is one of the founding members of the Dominican Republic network and the El Camino Network. Its role as a model ministry has inspired many throughout the country.

Currently two pastors in Chile, members of the El Camino Network, are developing plans for the formation of a national Chilean network. This year we plan to offer workshops to leaders who have shown interest in local church-based community development. The El Camino Network connects with a network in Costa Rica where a national consultation on holism was recently held. As we continue to identify models throughout the continent we will seek to accompany and encourage them towards the formation of local networks that strengthen the mission and expand the vision in their own contexts.

The El Camino Network is excited about what can be done throughout our continent through local churches committed to the practice of integral mission in their respective communities. Ultimately we recognize that this movement is God's. It reflects his heart and design for his bride, the local church. We contribute what God has blessed us with – our experiences, resources, passion and gifts – in order to further the cause. We believe that the local church is the hope of the world, and we want to help to make this radical statement a reality in Latin America.

Part Two

Integral Mission and the Poor

Integral Mission and the Practitioner's Perspective

Saul and Pilar Cruz

Walking Alongside the Poor: a Christian Possibility of Integral Mission

This paper reflects the main issues we have been experiencing and learning through our work alongside the poor for the last 13 years. When we started Armonia Ministries at the Jalalpa Ravine, a place of desperate poverty in Mexico City, we had to put into practice what resonated in our ears as integral mission among the poor. There were few material means to start with, although over the years we received the help of Tearfund, Armonia UK Trust, Orangewood Presbyterian Church of America and many other friends. From the very beginning it was an attempt at a fresh and contextual response, in flesh and blood, to questions about the gospel in terms of its relationship with the world, Christ's body, the poor and our responsibility towards them in Mexico City.

Our work exists inside a hermeneutic circle of reflection and action that begins its movement, direction and emphasis with questions inspired by the tradition of the International Fellowship of Evangelical Students (IFES), the ideas of numerous spiritual parents and the important lifetime work of John Stott, both in his books and through The London Institute for Contemporary Christianity, which he founded. These help us to explore ways to construct a bridge of relevant and meaningful dialogue between the Bible and our worlds.

Walking alongside the poor became the purpose of our lives out of obedience to Christ, compassion for the needy and feelings of holy indignation when we see that beings like us, created in the image of God, have to survive under humiliating conditions. We began by wondering how Jesus' words could become a reality among the poor of our day. How would it be possible for the new humanity in Christ to show his compassion to a world in need? How could we give evidence in an intelligent, contemporary, embodied and significant way of God's compassion; of our obedience; of our prophetic responsibilities; of true love? How will justice, respect, harmony, co-operation and an infinite number of other yearnings of God towards the needy ever be seen in our city, our country and our world?

The Contemporary Church and Jesus

To describe our ideas and ways of working we have to begin by pointing out the obvious difference between the total knowledge and wisdom of God and our limited knowledge. We acknowledge the difference between the perfect revelation of God in our Lord Jesus Christ and our limitations in understanding due to our cultural constructs and the beliefs that we sustain. It is the difference between the work of the Holy Spirit and our limited obedience.

We affirm, therefore, that we have a very limited and imperfect knowledge of this world. We as individuals in our processes of constructing descriptions of the world are bound by the beliefs and premises that exist in our world.

Therefore, our work as practitioners was not based on great knowledge and a clear, preconceived approach. It was made as we learned to walk with those the Lord gave us the privilege of loving in the slums of our city. And as such it is based on a hermeneutic circle of reflection and action. Thus we have come to understand that we relate to communities (as to the word and to God himself) through an understanding that modifies our relationship with those communities. We consider that practitioners construct, through their own understanding and descriptions, the interactive processes in which they are involved.

So we had to begin by doing something with the differences we could observe between Jesus' actions in the gospel and the church's actions in our day. There were, of course, many areas of concurrence, but on observing the narratives of what Christ did, such as in Matthew 9:31–35, one is surprised by Jesus' extraordinary actions. We see a compassionate Jesus going through towns and villages with open eyes, while today's church continues mostly trying to attract people – sometimes only to their local subculture – by means of all kinds of attractions in desperate, temple-centred activities. We see Jesus active every day, in contrast to a Sunday-centred church. In contrast to an unbalanced church that chooses to emphasize only some aspects of the gospel, we see Jesus in perfect balance: teaching, preaching and healing. And while we are in disagreement and in endless discussion on what to do for the downtrodden, we see Jesus harmoniously preaching to the human spirit, educating people and healing their bodies. We do not see Jesus devoted to the formation of experts in people's problems, but rather to the formation of disciples. We see him training people of faith who will work following his principles when faced with similar problems, but in different times and places. We see Jesus educating faithful people who can take in prayer to the Father what their eyes and their hearts tell them of the vast problems of the harassed and helpless among them. people who dare to pray that the work of God may be done among us.

We kept wondering if it was possible to ask the Lord of the harvest to give us, today, renovated eyes, hearts and hands to be his contemporary disciples. Was it possible to integrate the hermeneutic tradition with an approach in which the practitioner–community relationship is our main preoccupation? Can we be emancipated from the perspective of the missionary work of the 1950s and learn to be compassionate Christians and a transforming presence in this contemporary world? This is not meant disrespectfully. The 1950's idea of taking the church elsewhere was noble, necessary and revolutionary. The problem is that over the years it has become stagnant, distorted and anachronistic. It basically became the notion of bringing people to a temple on Sundays to re-educate them in the elements of the kingdom of God in heaven and our citizenship in it without emphasizing the prayer of Jesus for the kingdom of God to come to earth so that its transformational powers are among us. It became a practice in which Christian service was relegated to meeting-centred, member-only activities and only in a few cases proclamation, education and service to the whole surrounding community. It became the detachment of thought and compassion, of eyes and hearts and of hearts and hands.

Many practitioners like us, who started from pragmatic, classic or programmatic backgrounds, are now in the middle of a transitional phase. We are attempting to integrate old and new perspectives – certainties of basic Reformation Christianity with new sets of premises about our present-day responsibilities and ways of being involved in this process. What we have observed in the field raises questions that do not merely pertain to community intervention programmes. Instead they challenge the very notion of work among the poor and the identity of the practitioner. It is, in fact, a way of thinking that questions the foundations on which our understanding of the divine commission is based and questions the way in which we put it into practice.

As a consequence, we are trying to develop a perspective on learning and relating to the community that questions the traditional premises that define practitioners. In this transition, we have found ourselves faced with a number of challenges. These include:

1. a questioning of the traditional goals of community facilitators, workers, practitioners and missionaries towards which traditional community work was developed
2. a demystification of the practitioner's transformational skills
3. a consideration of which voices should participate in the community transformation process

1. Questioning Goals

Considering the first challenge – questioning the traditional goals of community work – we have come to question the nature of the relationship between practitioners or missionaries and the poor community members that is implicit in the goals of traditional church-related community work. Traditionally, a dualistic and hierarchical relationship is emphasized and in an implicit way the practitioner's culture is the ideal. As such it is assumed that the practitioner's culture does not need any kind of transformation. The practitioner is seen as the person who understands human needs and the one who dictates how development should occur. The traditional approach tells us that the cure of all disadvantage is linked to the precise identification of what is wrong. This cause of disadvantage should be destroyed or changed with a suitable programme. Under these assumptions the practitioner is a programme expert who has all the answers. Therefore the practitioner leads the practitioner–poor community member relationship. He or she will determine what the correct variety of experiences are, the kind of abilities community members should have and what the desired results are.

2. Demystifying the Practitioner's Skills

Our reflection on the second challenge – the need to demystify the practitioner's skills – has led us to the conclusion that you cannot impose values. Plans, possible programmes and even personal behaviour should be considered from a relational perspective without favouring one description, explanation or understanding above any other. This is usually the opposite of the basis upon which encounters between the practitioner and poor community members usually take place and on which the practitioners base their actions. It is, in fact, in acute contrast to the somehow generally accepted notion that concedes to churches, agencies or practitioners the power to change clients through their use of technical tools and financial resources.

Sometimes people think that the poor think little or not at all. The fact is that their thinking is undervalued. They think just the same as anybody else does and should have the opportunity to be heard and to enrich us:

> Do not think of yourself more highly than you should. Instead, be modest in your thinking, and judge yourself according to the amount of faith that God has given you. We have many parts in the one body, and all these parts have different functions (Rom. 12:3b–4, GNB).

All community and individual behaviours are a function of their cognitive and symbolic processes. Their interpersonal behaviours cannot be considered mere responses to what others do. These thinking processes are not absent because of the absence of food or resources. That is why they have their own values, what we call 'the culture of the poor'. The practitioner's interventions through activities, technology or programmes, then, do not have a transformational effectiveness in themselves since the practitioner's efforts are linked to the way in which the community members interpret his or her actions. Therefore for many years we had to learn how to construct new relationships in love and trust. A bridge of mutual trust, confidence and support is necessary and we suggest that three elements help in the building of this:

a. The non-verbal but unique power of compassionate love

A genuine preoccupation with community priorities and concerns was the initial element of our communication. That demanded, of course, an extensive investment of time and resources in others, rather than in the construction of our own buildings and responding to our organizational needs. This led us all to a mutual trust. Through this stage many believed in the love of Jesus, but it was not enough.

b. *The construction of a common language*

In spite of its imperfection, we use our language to create and recreate our relationships and our conception of our worlds. So in our encounters with the community we use language to create shared perceptions of realities and relationships. We are trying to stop emphasizing any hierarchical difference between us and freely open ourselves up to listen to the ideals of the kingdom alongside their descriptions, understandings and local meanings. All these practices produce a possibility of change and new knowledge for the other and for ourselves. More people were becoming Christians, but it was not enough.

c. *A common space for communal reflection*

We all created a common space for communal reflection – what we call 'a space for transformation'. This common space is a space where we could meet – no longer 'us and them', but all together. We understood that we needed relational conversations, not classic teaching. We needed a mutual effort to transform – *in the context of the word of God* – ourselves, the local culture and all the multiple possibilities for perceiving responsibility: love, suffering, crisis, family life, children, elderly people, sex, money, food, supporters, service to others, friendship, music, art, the indigenous people, education, politics, the Bible, our devotional life, the Father, the Son, the Holy Spirit and so on. These do not constitute a syllabus in the usual way, but are the expression of our interests. In the midst of these conversations, thanks to our dear Lord, transformation started to occur in very powerful ways.

3. Participation in Transformation

The third challenge is to consider which voices should participate in the community transformation process. Transformation occurs in the context of interaction. God has given us a foundation by communicating with us through his word and the myriad of different methods he employs to convey his plans, love and desires for his people. So, as human beings interact – with God and one another – he inspires us to share our part in this diversity through our different voices: the words, colours, songs, rhythms and languages he has given us in his greatness, mercy and transforming power. The possibilities are infinite and exhilarating as in God there is no fixed mode of body-wide behaviour, praise or worship. In Christ we have the potential to express and experiment with God's will. We can experiment with what is pleasing and perfect in our time, culture and location, time after time. In his body the voices of young and old, women and men, are harmonized to bear out the love made real in this world; the love that is a living sacrifice to God. Submission to God's will and expression of God's will are the voices that transform lives and transform communities.

But what are we to do with undesirable behaviour and thoughts that could undermine our communal life in Christ? We started a slow, but critical fight not just to substitute an undesirable value with its opposite, but instead to try to understand that change occurs through stability; that autonomy takes place through constraints; that freedom is only found through obedience; and that in limits we find possibilities. Without noticing, we stopped telling others who wanted to change their behaviour just to be the opposite of what they were. Instead we started to create possibilities together as we were discovering that we were members of the same body of Christ. As can be seen, these processes demand of the practitioner an attitude of humility, dependence on God and an intense learning process.

If the practitioner must be an expert in something it should not be the contents of people's lives so as to tell them how to be or what to do in every instance of life. Rather their expertise should be in the process of integral mission that starts in one's own eyes, heart, hands and mouth. They should enter into the process that in Christ moves back and forth from compassionate service to the formation of multiple relationships and possibilities for Christian transformation in the multiple dimensions of life. The practitioner's responsibility is primarily creating a space in which people can have significant relational conversations among themselves and with God. Integral mission, where the kingdom of God is brought into being in our social realities, relies upon this facilitating role of the practitioner.

It seems to us that the idea of a development agency or practitioner as an architect of change among the poor should be abandoned. When it comes to defining a community problem the true nature of the problem is rarely an external cause, such as the absence of water or means. In most cases poverty in a given community is related to the interpersonal and social dynamics that maintain the problem. If we observe carefully, problems appear in the way that people interact according to a series of values and beliefs. Their new interactions determine a series of beliefs, securities and behaviours that affect community life reciprocally. In that sense, called as we are to transformation among the poor in Christ's name, as practitioners we can define our role as that of participants and facilitators in the construction of interpersonal relationships based on the local and international, present and past, beliefs of Christ's body.

The Apostle Paul's teaching has been an extraordinary source of ideas for us on how this process of transformation can occur. Consider some critical ideas in Romans 12–15:

> Do not conform any longer to the pattern of this world, but be transformed by the renewing of your mind (Rom. 12:2).

> So in Christ we who are many form one body, and each member belongs to all the others (Rom. 12:5).

> For the kingdom of God is not a matter of eating and drinking, but of righteousness, peace and joy in the Holy Spirit, because anyone who serves Christ in this way is pleasing to God and approved by men. Let us therefore make every effort to do what leads to peace and to mutual edification (Rom. 14:17–19).

We have learned that we trigger a process of change in communities if we are successful in interfering with the cycle that keeps people locked in futile debate. But what does that mean? It seems to us that guidelines for practitioners could be identified as the following:

- a body of Christ challenge to the present, damaging ways of thinking through the introduction of differences: that is, real love, concern, service, sacrificial giving of time, resources, presence, gifts, interest and so on (not just an opposite to their current way of living)
- the proposal of different possibilities of living or of some event according to the power of salvation in Christ and the values of the kingdom of God
- new ways of connecting relationships, behaviours and events in the community

- the introduction of mutual interdependence as members of the same body

The intervention that introduces differences can only be the one that is 'recognized' as such by the community or member of it. Can we go as far as saying that no matter what the practitioner does, the result will always be determined by the community member's choice of what is useful for his or her change? People have even been given the freedom to resist or ignore the voice of God. We have to pay a lot of attention to this matter as we still do not understand how our conversations, histories, examples, readings and teachings are used by the Holy Spirit to bring about change. For example, what makes a relationship a process of correct, good and desirable learning? What gives a conversation an effect on other conversations? What makes a reading and a conversation around a story of the word of God become the point of reference for change for a person or a whole community?

Concluding Observations

Perhaps we could conclude with some intuitive observations from our interaction with the communities with whom we work.

We have to go to the poor if we want to meet them. It is not necessary to disguise ourselves as poor, but it is critical to form interactive relationships of trust for mutual transformation in the process of generating a new common language and new sets of common beliefs. Love is the fundamental way to communicate the desire of creating a common space for conversation, care and exploration of new possibilities for transformation.

Given an interactive relationship, the practitioner's questions, concrete examples, readings from the Bible, comments or the direct invitation for repentance of sins and the acceptance of Jesus Christ as Lord and Saviour challenge the coherence of the community member's values, descriptions, explanations, attributions and belief systems. This provokes a response from the community member – a reconsideration of their preconceptions.

Every time that an alternative Christian value, description, explanation or attribution is offered by the practitioner or a community member, the other members tend to integrate such possibilities into their belief systems. In a transforming relationship, a challenge to the community's held beliefs ruptures the coherence of their belief system and obliges the individuals to generate a new coherence that incorporates the new ideas. The most significant change in a community member's explanations, attributions and values occurs when a concrete example or believable account is given by the practitioner or by Christian members of the community to bear out their previously offered explanations and attributions. In this sense it is not sufficient solely to offer different points of view, it is also necessary that the Christian practitioner or the Christian community demonstrate the theory in practice.

Take, for example, Ephesians 4:28: 'If you are a thief, stop stealing. Begin using your hands for honest work, and then give generously to others in need' (NLT). This change is facilitated if the community members have experienced the possibility of generating different points of view.

All these processes take time, humility, patience and prayer. We learn as a community in the light of the Lord's infinite love and possibilities. And we pray that we can keep learning as we serve, walking alongside the poor, until he takes us to our eternal home.

Integral Mission with the Poor

Tim Costello

The inhabitants of London hear a familiar refrain as they disembark from their subway trains, so familiar that it is almost subliminal. But it certainly strikes first-time visitors when the doors open and the automated voice says 'mind the gap'. That gap between train and platform could be an image for the gap between evangelical faith and passionate engagement for the poor.

I discovered this gap between evangelical conviction and engagement on behalf of the poor when I moved from being the local Baptist minister to the elected mayor of the St Kilda Council. St Kilda is a suburb of Melbourne, Australia, known for its drugs, street prostitution and an entrenched divide between the wealthy and the poor. I stood on a platform of public housing for the poor and was proud to lead the first council in Australia to put local ratepayers' dollars into homelessness. Prior to this, housing had been a federal and state government responsibility with a shameful passing of responsibility and blame between these tiers of government that left the poor suffering and vulnerable. Now other councils throughout Australia have followed this lead.

But I also discovered that the committed support for my policies did not come from my evangelical or church comrades, but from secular groups. It caused me surprise and disappointment, and demonstrated a clear lack of integration. Since then it has been both a personal and theological question to ask why was this so.

I would like to consider this topic by reflecting on probably the most famous story Jesus told, colloquially called 'The Good Samaritan' (Lk. 10:25–37). This story was precipitated by two questions that highlight the gap between engagement with the poor and my evangelical upbringing. At first sight, the two questions seem so different and almost unrelated that one wonders if the Good Samaritan story is indeed a response to both.

What must I do to inherit eternal life?

The first question is: 'What must I do to inherit eternal life'? It is individualistic, self-referencing and acquisitive. It is, however, also an intensely spiritual question and was the dominant question of my evangelical tradition. Indeed, this question organized the priorities of my church and its passion.

The question you determine as fundamental reveals your fundamentals. The question you name as prior determines your priorities. Most Baptist churches, as I have experienced them, focus their spiritual energy into financial giving for evangelistic crusades, youth outreach, lay witness and church planting. To ask where this focused energy emanated from is to discover the fascination with this first question. Eternal life and the believer's assurance with heavenly security are what ultimately matter. Indeed, as a young evangelical, I was taught that there is no more awesome question that can be posed to our children, our loved ones, our neighbours and our world.

We carried the heavy responsibility for the eternal salvation or damnation of other people into every aspect of our lives. Practically, this meant at times I felt unable to take a holiday, focus on professional study or career or even relax and enjoy transient joys, as these things absorbed precious time and distracted from this most urgent eternal responsibility. I did not feel any comparable burden for the fate of those living in absolute and hopeless poverty. Theologically the paramount importance of this question relativized other parts of Scripture such as the Hebrew prophets, Matthew 25 and James's reflection on how faith without works was a sham salvation. They were somehow regarded as second-order teaching to inheriting eternal life.

Consequently, it seemed always disappointing to me, as an evangelical, that Jesus refused to answer the question posed by the religious lawyer. Of course, Luke tells us that the question was a test and I have come to realize that it is still a test for evangelicals. There has been many a time I have preached on this text and wished that Jesus gave a clear, simple, first-century Palestinian version of the four spiritual laws. What an opportunity he seemed to miss when today we can pray a lifetime for a non-Christian friend to ask us that precise question and most evangelicals die without anyone ever actually bothering.

Jesus throws the question back with a question: What does the Bible teach? This religious lawyer gives a magnificent summary of the Hebrew Law and prophets: love God intensely; love your neighbour as intensely as you love yourself. Jesus congratulates him, promises that he shall indeed live and turns to go. This is practically the point at which my evangelical tradition finished its theological enquiry. We read the second question, but failed to notice its relationship to this first question.

Simply put, it was relegated in priority to merely an expression of soteriology. Saved people were good people like the Good Samaritan, but they had to be saved first. The story became a quaint illustration of the dangers of travel on the Jerusalem–Jericho road, only intensifying my despair when I recognized my tradition's lack of an integrated gospel and passion for the poor. In short I received a world view that left a chasm between the spiritual and material; between justice and justification; between worship and politics; between jubilee teaching and economics; between forgiveness of sins and forgiveness of debts; and between evangelism and social action.

Who is my neighbour?

The second question is: 'Who is my neighbour'? It is communal, directed outward, self-surrendering and highly social. It is the organizing question of social justice and social compassion. When this question is prior, fundamental budgets, programmes and services reflect this priority. Of course, within the Christian church, Christian Aid, World Vision, TEAR Australia and many other organizations have arisen from this question.

It was this second unrehearsed and genuine question that drew the immediate response of the story of the Good Samaritan. It probably caused, however, this religious lawyer to wish he had never asked. By the end of the story his ethnic and religious categories were exploded. The very group he loathed and despised was now the central frame of his spiritual vision. He was dragged out of his comfort zones and forced to confront his deepest prejudices and religious coldness if he was to inherit eternal life.

Minding the Gap

These two questions still typify a yawning gap in the secular mind today. In Australia if you asked people to define a Christian or a religious person they would most probably say someone who loves God, who lives in this world but reflects more on the next, and whose worship and piety is to ready themselves for heaven. Such a person talks of being saved because their real energies are directed to their eternal fate.

Similarly, if you asked someone in Australia who a social reformer is, they are more likely to say that it is someone who has a love for their neighbour and who works hard, even slavishly, to transform and change the world now. They want to see salvation here and now. Their preoccupation is political and social transformation on this earth. The best-known secular 'saint' who has captured the imagination of Australians in recent years was Dr Fred Hollows. A professed atheist, albeit raised in a Church of Christ family, he rejected its other-worldly theology and went to work as an eye surgeon with Third World and Aboriginal peoples who suffered from cataracts and blindness. With his premature death just a few years ago there was an enormous outpouring of grief and the appending of the word 'saint' to this secularized doctor's life and mission.

But Jesus' response showed no gap between these questions. The story of the Good Samaritan is, indeed, a response to both queries. Future salvation and salvation now, expressed in a love of neighbour, belong together. The separation of these questions is one of the deepest failures of evangelicalism as a theological tradition. Jesus saw these two questions as indivisible – two sides of the one coin. To divide them was to render the gospel powerless and neutral. It was to do the opposite of releasing power by splitting the atom: it was to neutralize the power of the gospel and allow wealthy Christians to feel at ease in this world while blissfully certain of the next.

Evangelicals are not alone here. John Cornwell's book *Hitler's Pope*[59] reveals what may occur when these questions are separated. Cornwall documents how the future Pius XII, whose real name was Eugenio Pacelli, left defenceless Germany's 23 million Catholics in 1933, when he was a Vatican diplomat. In that year he signed a concordat with Hitler that agreed to disband the only democratic party left in Germany able to challenge Nazism, the Catholic Centre Party. He also agreed to withdraw Catholics from all social and political action. Their newspapers, their extensive associations with a political edge, such as Catholic Action, were all willingly surrendered. Why? In return for this withdrawal, the Catholic church was granted full religious freedom and given funding for all their teachers in Catholic schools. Pacelli, who had been seeking this concordat with the Weimar Republic even before Hitler took power, believed that the church's religious vocation was primary, and its political and social action was expendable.

After signing this concordat Hitler wrote, 'It seems to me to give sufficient guarantee that the Reich members of the Roman Catholic confession will from now on put themselves without reservation at the service of the new National Socialist State.' Before we feel too self-righteous we need to remember that Protestants soon followed with their own concordat based on similar principles.

The day after signing this 1933 concordat the Nazis began their boycott against Jewish businesses. This was the first major test on a national scale of the attitude of the

---

[59] John Cornwell, *Hitler's Pope: The Secret History of Pius XII* (New York: Viking, 1999)

Christian church toward the situation of the Jews under the new Hitler government. Not a single word of protest was heard from the churches. Cardinal Faulbacher of Munich said: 'The Jews can help themselves.' In terms of the Good Samaritan, Catholics and Protestants under Hitler proved to be the priest and the Levite who saw the battered Jew lying vulnerable and defenceless on the Central European roadside.

But were the priest and Levite in Jesus' story just hard-hearted and uncaring? I doubt it. They simply had a focus on their spiritual and religious duties. If they bent down and helped this bruised and bleeding victim they would be rendered ceremonially unclean. They would fail their duties in the Temple, the synagogue and to the faithful. The clash of priorities between religious and social responsibilities outweighed the personal and humane responsibilities of citizenship to a fellow Jew, not to mention common neighbourliness. Their immediate deference to the religious priority impeded them crossing the cultic boundaries of clean and unclean that were the touchstone of Jewish holiness. Just as in the 1930s, when Catholic priests and Protestant leaders passed on by, the theological articulation of religious priorities and spiritual attentiveness produced unjust and incomprehensible results.

Bridging the Gap

A passion for souls must proceed from a passion for the poor and therefore spiritual and social involvement is an expression of the same gospel. Indeed, the passion for evangelism must be seen as stemming from the same holy motivation as to love our neighbours as ourselves. Evangelism without neighbourly love that sees brokenness and injustice is a spiritualized form of a privatized gospel. It is caricatured by those who hear our preaching as akin to selling tickets to the great concert in the sky, where those who respond can have the assurance that their entrance is guaranteed and seat secure. But equally, social action and justice without evangelism is a recipe for burnout, dryness and disillusionment. We are saved and changed in order to change our world. Loving our neighbour and loving God belong together if we are to know eternal life.

Only by overcoming the gap between these two questions and seeing them fused as one will we ensure an evangelical integration of good news for the poor. The more the questions are separated for theological or strategic reasons, the greater the corresponding loss of integration and integrity. Evangelists with lasting impact understood this integration. Charles Finney, the great American evangelist of the nineteenth century, was said to have the greatest retention rate from those who were converted through his preaching. Yet it was Finney who refused to offer the sacraments to slave owners, even though they boasted impeccable born-again credentials. It was Finney who scandalized society by training the first black people and women for ministry at Oberlin College.

Many of the other evangelical heroes have the same integration in the outworking of their faith. At age 26 the English social reformer, William Wilberforce, thought he would leave Parliament and become a clergyman in order to have a truly spiritual ministry. But John Newton wrote to him, urging him to stay in politics and telling him his calling was in the secular field. Wilberforce renounced the illusion that only pursuing the first question – 'What must I do to inherit eternal life?' – could lead to a truly spiritual vocation and spent the next 51 years of his life fighting slavery. John Wesley preached 'social holiness' that integrated atonement and social transformation and William Booth challenged the church of his day's apathy and blindness with his book *In Darkest England And The Way Out* (1890).

I expect these evangelical leaders would challenge the church today to commit to social action *and* evangelism, lay witness *and* advocacy, prayer *and* jubilee economics, worship *and* politics as expressions of the gospel. Then, along with our trademark evangelistic programmes, we might be equally known for leading anti-capitalism demonstrations instead of leaving it to anarchists and radicals. We would practise non-violence in such demonstrations, but like the Good Samaritan we would refuse to ignore the smashed-up neighbourhoods of our world because the IMF (International Monetary Fund) and World Bank assure us that they are doing all that is possible to help the poor. These demonstrations have exposed that the daily violence of 40,000 children dying from preventable diseases represents a total failure of their policies. They also unmask the Western, liberal media's shocked outrage that a Nike shop or McDonald's was defaced to make this systemic evil visible. These demonstrations have shocked the élites and reminded them that the failure of their political and spiritual imagination is noticed. Curiously it has helped the IMF and World Bank to remember that they actually exist to solve these problems.

At the heart of the gospel is the fact that God loves us and sent his Son to die for us. We only learn to love through the love of others. One of the quickest ways to make prisoners and asylum seekers morally invisible to their guards is to deny them visits from their loved ones, thereby ensuring that the guards never see them through the eyes of those who love them. The power of the story of the Good Samaritan is that eternal life is linked to One who refuses to avert the eyes, who refuses to look away and thus not have to love. Even a defence of the priority of the spiritual dimension is demolished, as neighbourly love is the evidence of eternal life. This is a God big enough for the pain of this world and a gospel integral to the poor. This gospel remains a challenge theologically and practically for the evangelical church.

Case Study

Empowering Rural Communities: Mara and Ukerewe Diocese, Tanzania

Bishop Peter Kitula

Overview

Organization
Diocese of Mara and Ukerewe of the Africa Inland Church Tanzania

Project description
Developing church-based integral mission in a rural context

Issues
Rural development, participation and empowerment, church-based development, capacity building, integral mission

Context

The Diocese of Mara and Ukerewe of the Africa Inland Church Tanzania (AICT) was formed in November 1993. From the beginning the church took seriously the need to address the social problems within the diocese. In many of the then 12 pastorates (there are now 23) Bishop Peter Kitula was asked by the village leaders, some of whom were not Christians, for the diocese to consider alleviating the social needs. Communities pointed to the need for good health, safe drinking water, quality education and food security. Requests were made, for example, for grinding machines, so that women would no longer need to walk up to 10 kilometres to a grinder carrying 20 kilograms of grain, often along with their baby.

In response to these requests the diocese tried to write proposals to funding agencies. Not much was achieved, however, perhaps because the diocese lacked the capacity to write and implement project proposals. The church in the diocese did not understand itself well, or the magnitude of the problems.

In 1996 the bishop invited the Christian Organizations Research Advisory Trust (CORAT) to conduct an assessment and make long-term plans for development projects. CORAT helped the diocese identify its vision, mission and values together with a five-year strategic plan. CORAT contacted Tearfund UK, which had been a friend of AICT Mara and Ukerewe since 1994 through support of a small evangelistic project. Tearfund UK and the diocese agreed to form a partnership with the facilitation of an independent consultant.

The diocese and Tearfund UK agreed in 1997 that instead of starting sustainable development programmes with the entire diocese, they would start with five of the ten poorest pastorates: Isenye, Kasuguti, Kabasa, Tarime and Nansio. From these, seven villages were identified: Kitembele and Wegete (Isenye); Ragata (Kasuguti); Kabasa (Kabasa); Utegi (Tarime), and Muluseni and Hamuyebe (Nansio).

Despite the diversity of tribes in Mara and Ukerewe, there are noticeable cultural similarities between these villages. There are strong ties in the communities because many families are neighbours with their extended families. Everyone knows most of the other villagers by name. In each village there are a few churches including Roman Catholic, Seventh-Day Adventist and a small percentage of evangelicals like AICT, but the majority of the people have no affiliation to these churches. At a crisis like prolonged sickness, the death of a loved one, barrenness or rejection in marriage, the people turn to the occult, seeking the aid of diviners or magicians. Few, if any, deny the supernatural.

The people are economically poor. Most live in grass thatched huts and use logs for chairs. Women fetch water from a common village well, some walking up to three miles. The people live on food grown and processed by themselves. In some villages people get fish from Lake Victoria while in others women gather vegetables that grow naturally in the fields. In Kitembele and Wegete some get dried meat from poachers who kill the wildlife of the Serengeti National Park.

Some people believe their poverty to be caused by bad people who magically prevent rain. The solution is to go to rainmakers. Though the rainmakers show no apparent success, it is considered better to try than to be passive. The real causes of poverty include ignorance, poor agricultural inputs, natural calamities, underutilization of the local resources, low capital for investment, poor or no planning, people's perception of poverty as normal, laziness, disease, lack of motivation and poor infrastructure.

Description

In partnership with Tearfund UK the diocese came up with an integrated mission programme. The major objective was to minister to the poor, showing them the love of God through his church, improving their standard of living by assisting them in sustainable development within their communities and presenting them the gospel of Jesus Christ. The development projects that have been implemented as a result of the process involve health, education and safe drinking water programmes. The diocese used the 'Participatory Evaluation Process' (PEP) as a strategy for conducting community mobilization. The PEP strategy involved calling people together in the seven communities and, with the help of consultants, having the people themselves identify needs and solutions. In each village the mobilization was done by four 'Community Owned Resource Persons' (CORPS), two of whom were representatives of the church.

Other activities were done concurrently with PEP. These included football (soccer) matches between a diocesan team, including the consultants, and community teams. During break a brief gospel presentation or testimony was given. At night gospel films, including the famous 'Jesus film', were shown to the village.

In order to have a more powerful Christian witness the evangelism department of the diocese planned evangelistic outreaches in the target communities. After beginning the day with prayer, some team members visit homes while others conduct a seminar for new believers. In the afternoon there is an evangelistic crusade and counselling for new converts, with gospel films at night. The diocesan team works with the local church and follow-up is usually undertaken by local Christians who are trained prior to the campaign.

Results

The results have been very encouraging in a number of ways. Physical transformation has taken place. At Lagata the community has built two classrooms and four houses for teachers at the local primary school. Before the programme both the administrators of the school and the community were waiting passively for the government to do the work. At Kabasa two new wells have been constructed and six old traditional wells have been restored. A new primary school is under construction. At Kitembele a secondary school with four classrooms, two houses for teachers and a dispensary have been constructed. At Wegete a dispensary and a well have been build and at Utegi the community has started the construction of a dispensary. A primary school is under construction in Hamuyebe, which has also become the chief supplier of vegetables in the region. At Muluseni the community had been waiting for the Ministry of Education to build a roof on a classroom. Now the community itself has roofed it, built a house for the head teacher and the foundations for three further classrooms.

In these projects the seven communities provided 90 per cent of the resources with only about 10 per cent coming from the diocese. And there have been additional blessings. At Lagata, for example, people mobilized by the CORPS organized themselves to restore their plunge dip for washing their cattle. At Kitembele the people built tanks for harvesting rain water from public buildings.

These efforts were not part of the original plan, but are an extension of the principles learned through the programme.

With the building of the schools children can go to school without the constant demand of money for the building fund. Clean drinking water has meant the reduction of water-borne diseases. For the poor who lack money for treatment these diseases were often life-threatening. When the dispensaries are operational this will further increase their lifespan.

There have been positive spiritual results. People are more open to what the church has to say than they used to be. Friendship has been built between the church and the people in the communities. At Utegi the village government supported the Utegi evangelistic outreach with beans and chickens for the evangelists' meals. When I visited Utegi and Kabasa the village government provided the goats for the meals.

More important is the conversion of the unbelievers. Membership has increased in our churches in these communities. The village chairman of Kabasa gave his life to Jesus Christ during one of the evangelistic crusades. Some months later, while at the Bunda Church Conference, I had the joy of baptizing him and other new believers from Kabasa. The unity of the church has also been noted. Christians who come to the training seminars find it rewarding to join together in fellowship as they learn and serve together.

The programme has been an agent of change culturally and socially. People have discovered how much can be accomplished when people come together. Relationships among the villagers have improved. During recent elections leaders who were actively involved in our community meetings were elected. Candidates referred to their involvement in the development programme.

Instead of attributing disease and death to witchcraft, some of the people are now seeing that their 'witches' are unsafe water and poor sanitation. People in villages that have modern wells are not suffering from water-borne disease, as they used to. People are seeing the real causes of disease and death.

People's understanding of the causes of poverty has only partially been transformed – it is an ongoing process. But, seeing what planning and a determination not to accept the *status quo* can do, they are beginning to believe that they do not have to accept poverty as a normal way of life.

Impact

Before embarking on this programme church people had a dichotomized approach to serving. The church's role was seen as ministering only to the soul. An holistic approach was not practised. Now, after seeing how receptive unbelievers have been to an integrated approach, some of the church people are accepting that their mission is to serve people in their totality. The evangelism department of the diocese has conducted two seminars on biblical holism (February and April 2001). In both cases church leaders were keen to start holistic ministries in their areas.

The attitude of communities towards the church is positive. The church is now seen not as an institution 'doing their own thing', but rather as an agent of change, transforming lives both physically and spiritually.

The church is continuing to pursue the goal of helping people deal with the enemy of poverty and its causes through consultancy. We believe that as people interact with experts on issues like modern farming techniques, quality education, good health and planning, poverty will continue to decrease.

While the church has grown considerably, growth could be faster if some of the challenges were addressed. The diocese still has a limited capacity to assign qualified pastors and evangelists to all the target areas. We need to mobilize and motivate the Christians, especially in those areas, to study for pastoral ministry and place them back in their own communities to serve their people. The problem is that many young Christian people who finish secondary school do not want to train for the ministry for fear that they will not be paid enough to live on.

Relationships between groups have grown. The villages that are involved in water projects have built good relations with Health Sanitation and Water Programme (HESAWA) workers. The churches have a better relationship with the diocese. The consultants have made friends with diocesan staff and church people in the target communities. Because the consultants are Christians, they have preached or witnessed in the communities during village meetings, games, film shows and evangelistic crusades. They are even counted as associate members of those churches.

The regional and district government leaders have also benefited. The changes are reported as 'progress in their areas'. At Lagata the Bunda District Commissioner promised to provide a truck to transport timber next time educational buildings are constructed. At Utegi the District Office provided a truck to bring sand to a building site.

Evaluation

Despite its success there are factors that continue to work against the programme. Some people still have the 'do it for me' or 'give me' mentality – training needs to be continually repeated. The diocese lacks the capacity to minister more effectively – the development department only consists of one person. External factors like droughts push our efforts back. The diocese needs to involve local churches more in the target communities to increase the spiritual impact.

Nevertheless, looking back, we have found that when we facilitate communities to find solutions to their own needs, people have a real sense of ownership of the projects that follow and implementation becomes easier. We have to be patient because development can be a slow process, using a lot of time, resources and talents. But changes that take place from within through a change of attitude are more permanent and more sustainable.

Case Study

Community-Based Urban Health:
Servants to Asia's Urban Poor, Cambodia

Janet Cornwall and Susan Jack

Overview

Organization
Servants to Asia's Urban Poor, Cambodia

Project description
An integrated community health programme among the urban poor

Issues
Peer education, mobilizing community volunteers, urban development, community health, HIV/AIDS, integral mission

Context

Cambodia has a population of approximately eleven million, one million of whom live in the capital, Phnom Penh. After a five-year civil war, the Khmer Rouge, led by Pol Pot, came to power in 1975. The following three years are well known as those of the 'killing fields'. During this time at least two million people were killed or died from illness or starvation. The destructive legacy of this loss of a generation of educated people and the total breakdown of civil society has proved long lasting. Following Vietnamese intervention in 1978, Cambodia was closed to the Western world until elections in 1993. In 1997 Hun Sen, the second Prime Minister, gained control in a coup and continued in power after 1999 elections. These political events continue to cause tension.

The Cambodian nation is, by definition, Theravada Buddhist. The Vietnamese, the largest other ethnic group, are either Mahayana Buddhist or Catholic. There are also significant communities of Cham Muslims, including one in the Servants' target area.

HIV/AIDS was first reported in Cambodia in the early 1990s and was predicted to be the worst epidemic in Asia. It is encouraging that recent data shows a downward trend in seroprevalence. However the number of people developing AIDS and dying continues to rise, creating a rapidly increasing demand for AIDS care and treatment. Surveys conducted in 2000 suggest that there has been no improvement in recent years in wider health indicators. One in eight Cambodian children will die before their second birthday. Vaccination rates are low at 40 per cent. Maternal mortality rate is 541 in every 100,000 live births. Economic growth rates are below what the Asia Development Bank estimates are required to affect poverty and projected growth rates have had to be revised downwards after recent flooding, which affected 2.7 million people.

Description

Since 1993 Servants has been contracted with the Ministry of Health to support community health services in Mean Chey District, Phnom Penh, which has a population of 160,000 people. Initially support was give to the government health centre, but now this support is limited to its community outreach components. For the most part Servants work independently to target healthcare interventions to the most vulnerable and marginalized. Work includes:

Child health:	community nutrition; children with disability; immunization; children at risk from HIV/AIDS; health education; sanitation in schools
Women's health:	savings and credit co-operative; birth spacing and antenatal care; commercial sex worker outreach; traditional birth attendant training
Public health:	HIV/AIDS education and homecare; support to the government TB programme; community sanitation

Throughout the district Servants has an extensive network of community contacts including women's association members, group leaders and community volunteers. It is our desire to see impacts multiplied by mobilizing community resources at all these levels. Another important component of Servants ministry is the desire of the expatriate team to live in the communities we work among in an attempt to become insiders rather than outsiders. Over time we have been learning how to balance idealism with personal needs in order to develop sustainable lifestyles. While this strategy is at times difficult and not necessarily the most efficient way to do project work, it remains a key part of our ministry here and is responsible for much of our impact.

Our work with HIV/AIDS started in 1995 following the formation of the National AIDS Programme as a division of the Ministry of Health. Servants workers Sue Jack and Mam Savath were involved in the first HIV/AIDS day commemoration in 1995. Community education started in response to a request by a Muslim leader for education. The objective was to raise awareness among the community about HIV transmission and prevention, with the hope that this would lead to sustained behaviour change: in particular the decrease in men visiting commercial sex workers and taking the infection home to their wives. After three years' general community education the thrust has moved to higher risk groups: young people (students and unemployed) and factory workers. The aim has been to encourage people to share their knowledge with others by training peer educators. A second thrust has been to create positive peer pressure and positive youth subcultures by working with church youth groups and emphasizing values such as abstinence, faithfulness and love. The third component of the HIV/AIDS prevention programme has been education and healthcare in the local sex workers' area. At the start of the outreach in 1996 there was almost no use of condoms and a high proportion of ulcerating sexually transmitted diseases. There has been a dramatic and sustained change in both these indicators.

Care for people affected by HIV/AIDS started in 1996. Community carers were recruited from those already known to be involved in care. Local churches were approached for interested people. Community carers receive a small stipend for their work, enough to compensate them for loss of earnings – all are poor and have to work to eat for the day.

Following on the care of adults with HIV/AIDS has been the need to care for children. The programme provides counselling and care for mothers and children affected by HIV/AIDS. The aim is to decrease mother-to-child transmission of HIV and provide medical care and nutritional support to those affected. We plan care for AIDS orphans by preparing families for fostering and provide support for relatives caring for extended family members.

Servants also provides technical assistance and training to a number of Christian groups and churches to help increase awareness about HIV/AIDS and compassionate care for those living with the disease.

Results

The findings of a recent external evaluation demonstrated that the programmes are having a major positive impact on the quality of life of chronically ill patients and their families in Mean Chey District. The vast majority of these are living in conditions of abject poverty, as Servants successfully target the poorest sections of the community.

There has been a significant improvement at a number of levels. High-quality clinical and community-based medical care has improved the health status of the chronically ill, including those with HIV/AIDS and TB. The hygiene status, nutritional status and quality of life of patients, families and caregivers have improved with reduction of stress and anxiety through the provision of systematic ongoing nursing care, health education, compassionate counselling and emotional support. Prevention has improved through health education to targeted groups. Monitoring, food supplements and medication have improved the health status of children and children's lives have been saved. The poorest and most disadvantaged individuals and families in the community have been empowered.

Impact

Perhaps the best way to describe the impact of the programme on individual lives and the local church is to give some case histories of community volunteers and people affected by HIV/AIDS. While problems are not over by any means, there is evidence of change and hope.

Yay Navy was an alcoholic, but when she became a Christian through a Khmer church she stopped drinking and has became a vibrant witness in her community. She and her husband have a house church in their home each Sunday, which two Servants staff help to facilitate. Mainly through Yay Navy's witness, membership has grown from two families to more than twenty over the last two years. They live in a squatter area that floods each year, washing in the city sewage and factory effluent. Yay Navy has cared for 18 neighbours with HIV/AIDS, many of them coming to know the love of Jesus because of her witness. She has recently taken in two orphans of a neighbour who died of HIV/AIDS.

Neang is 20 years old. She lives with five members of her extended family in a bamboo house in a slum area. Recent flooding has left the house falling apart. Her mother earns approximately one US dollar each day selling cakes. Apart from Neang's stipend from homecare visits, the family has no other source of income. Neang had to leave school after three years because the family could not afford to continue her education. However, she is bright and has ambitions to become a nurse. Neang has been working as a volunteer for over a year and is now also working half-time helping the Servants' AIDS homecare programme staff. She likes the work as she wants to help people, especially the very poor. In her work she provides physical care, bathing patients, cleaning and dressing wounds. Neang is an active member of her local church and leads a cell group in her village. She is keen to share her love of Jesus with the people for whom she cares.

Heng is a 37-year-old mother with 3 children. She and her husband, Ly, live in a crowded slum area by the river. Both Heng and Ly have AIDS. The couple are extremely poor and their only source of income is Ly's work as a porter and bicycle driver, for which he earns 50–75 US cents each day. Their extended family has stopped visiting and supporting Ly and Heng. The couple now receive regular home visits from Servants staff and volunteers. Heng and Ly acknowledge the material and medical support, but say that what they appreciate most is the opportunity to talk about their problems with people who really care. The volunteer who visited Heng and Ly from the time of their diagnosis with AIDS took them to a local church – their first-ever visit to a church. As a result they have become Christians and gain encouragement from their new faith. The children are being cared for by the church orphanage, but also come home regularly. Thanks to the homecare visits, Ly sometimes is well enough to earn some money and Heng is trying to re-establish her business. Discrimination from neighbours is less, Ly has stopped visiting sex workers, drinking alcohol and smoking, and they are both following advice on hygiene and nutrition.

Srey Phalla was widowed and then abandoned by her second husband. Her family was poor and had no place for her so Phalla came to Phnom Penh with her two daughters and newborn son. In a not uncommon scenario, she ended up in prostitution. To get through the day she would drink cheap rice wine. Phalla's first husband's family was concerned about the girls and took them away early on. In 1999 she told our staff at our weekly clinic that she wanted to leave prostitution. They were able to arrange a place at a YWAM (Youth With A Mission) shelter where she spent six months. During this time she stopped drinking and became a Christian. At the end of the six months she returned to the brothel area, but sold fruit instead. Phalla continued to attend church and has been baptized. She was, and remains, a wonderful witness to other women in a similar situation. Unfortunately after about four months she became ill with TB and AIDS and was found squatting at the hospital, cared for by her six-year-old son. Servants then placed Phalla in a hospice and care was arranged for her son. She is now enjoying relatively good health and sees her son regularly. Her son thrived in the loving atmosphere of the small homely orphanage and started school. Phalla commented on how he is now less angry, and more gentle and kind. Recently a permanent home has been found for him, bringing great joy to both him and his mother.

Evaluation

Peer education

While large numbers of people have been reached directly by the community education programme, the effectiveness of those trained as peer educators is low. It is planned to consolidate the existing peer education programme for students, high-risk groups and factory workers by providing a longer period of initial formal training to new peer educators. More time will be spent on improving the trainees' knowledge base, confidence and communication skills. Difficult concepts will be reinforced with ongoing refresher training, support and supervision.

Homecare volunteers

Training people who have little or no formal education is difficult and needs intensive and ongoing coaching and revision. A greater degree of support in the form of meetings, picnics and informal contacts has improved the morale and motivation of volunteers. Trying to improve co-operation and networking between volunteers in different areas is an ongoing aim in order to strengthen relationships, decrease dependence on Servants staff and reduce the vulnerability of the programme to volunteer dropout.

Church and community

Links with local churches and community representatives have been mostly informal and some of these resources are thus neglected. Initial meetings have been held with church leaders and key community leaders, but then ongoing contact has been informal. We are beginning to establish more systematic linkages with church groups and community representatives through regular meetings.

Case Study

Drug and Alcohol Rehabilitation: Teen Challenge, Kazakstan

Douglas Boyle

Overview

Organization
Teen Challenge, Kazakstan

Project description
Drug and alcohol rehabilitation

Issues
Addiction, rehabilitation, discipleship, church planting, integral mission

Context

Teen Challenge, Kazakstan (TCK) is a drug and alcohol rehabilitation programme in Almaty, Kazakstan, operating under the banner of Teen Challenge International. Teen Challenge began in 1959 with the work of David Wilkerson among young people in New York who were involved in drug addiction and criminal gangs. Today there are more than 150 Teen Challenge centres in 53 countries.

The programme is a biblically based method of drug and alcohol rehabilitation through which people come to a saving knowledge of Jesus and are discipled and prepared for kingdom service. Teen Challenge sees addiction not as a sickness, but as a crime against God, against oneself, against family and against society. Drug addiction is a deliberate choice made by individuals. Accepting personal responsibility for addiction is essential for change. Addiction destroys a person physically, intellectually, emotionally, socially and spiritually. For rehabilitation to be permanent it must produce positive change in all these areas. Change is gradual as students learn by training and experience to solve life's problems positively and to live without drugs.

Formally part of the Soviet Union, Kazakstan is now part of the Commonwealth of Independent States (CIS). Seventy per cent of the population is Muslim. Poverty in Kazakstan is primarily a result of the breakdown of the Soviet system. The country has gone from being a welfare state to one with virtually no welfare. Many of the social institutions, such as hospitals, kindergartens, schools and orphanages have closed because what was free now has to be paid for. The population was not equipped to cope with these unexpected changes. Kazakstan has an official employment rate of less than 20 per cent, but probably more like 70 per cent of the population have an income of some kind.

Drug use is part of the history of Kazakstan. The opium poppy is grown in the mountains and people have been using opium, in chewable form, for centuries. In more recent times, intravenous use of opium and the use of heroin have become prevalent. It is believed that this form of drug addiction touches 70 per cent of all families in Kazakstan across all economic and educational levels. Alcohol, particularly vodka, is a part of the cultural and social fabric of all the former Soviet states, and Mikhail Gorbachov identified it as the major cause of the collapse of the Soviet industrial machine.

At present drug addiction is seen as a disease. The drug addict is seen as a victim rather than an active decision maker and participant in his or her sin. This attitude is maintained within families – codependency is very common. In Kazakstan addicts remain with their families. As a result addicts put pressure on their families, shifting blame, deceiving and ultimately turning to theft and violence. Many families are forced to sell their homes to clear debts caused by the addict. Some find it difficult to work and many lose their jobs.

Description

Initially the main objective of the project was to free people from heroin addiction and to take them through a process of rehabilitation centred in Christian discipleship. Success is not just people freed from narcotic use, but people being trained as disciples of Jesus and serving him in some way.

The project started with a conference to identify the size of the need. TCK then worked with the local church to find programme workers and rent a rehabilitation centre. The 18-month residential training programme of the centre is the core of TCK's work. The programme is broken into four stages. The first stage (month 1) is *detoxification* – the physical withdrawal from drugs. The second stage (months 2–6) is *recovery* from the lifestyle of addiction. Students begin to engage in normal life without drugs or contact with addicted people. A disciplined daily routine of work, study, worship, play and sleep is established within the centre. Stage three (months 7–12) involves *solving life's problems*. Students learn to cope with daily life through problem solving and decision making. At this stage children come to live in the centre with their mothers and contact with family members increases. Stage four (months 13–18) is *re-entry*. Students prepare to leave the programme and learn to work for their own personal needs. They take work outside the centre and also accept the extra responsibility of supervising younger students.

The scope of the work of TCK has broadened over time to include a refuge for homeless women, children and those at risk of abuse; recovery programmes for family members; sporting clubs as part of the drug prevention programme; and a full academic school for child addicts, the children of addicts and those at risk.

The programme uses behavioural psychology, but within the framework of Christian discipleship. In looking for behavioural change the Bible is used as the rehabilitation manual. The programme is intensely spiritual. The day starts with prayer and there are five preaching times each day with an emphasis on developing a personal relationship with God. The programme involves attending a weekly cell group and a local church twice every Sunday. As the students progress through the programme they are encouraged to take part in a church ministry, such as children's church, choir or youth ministry. All the original workers came from the local church and had a heart to serve God in this ministry.

Results

Physical transformation in rehabilitation work can be seen within about eight weeks. The spiritual transformation takes longer as the new believers come to understand their new faith and come to terms with their own sin and personal attitudes. Slower still are the positive effects on the whole family. Families are now required to attend a Family Recovery Programme designed for their healing and development. This helps them understand the nature of their family member's addiction and the effect it has had on all those associated with him or her. When an addict stops using drugs everything changes within their family. Their lives no longer revolve around the addict, they are able to seek work and become involved in productive activities again.

The greatest evidence of spiritual transformation has been the planting of churches that are now having their own impact on the community. Eight churches have been planted out of the ministry and seven graduates are fully accredited pastors serving in churches. Many more are faithfully serving as deacons, worship leaders, children's church leaders and youth group leaders.

At the beginning there was tremendous hostility from government departments towards TCK because under the Soviet system the government provided all the welfare. But God rescued this situation. The fact that TCK has become the largest drug rehabilitation organization in Central Asia and that it is achieving its goals has really led to this transformation. The president has spoken about the programme and now recognizes that not all the social services of the country have to be provided by the government. The TCK school has obtained its registration and has started issuing the Kazakstan certificate for school-leavers.

TCK continues to face obstacles. The laws of Kazakstan do not allow anonymity, so the police would often break in to arrest people. To stop this, barbed-wire fences were built around our centres. There have been threats from prosecutors and the KGB. But the reputation of the programme has reduced the number of serious problems. The tax laws are also prohibitive and TCK has to have 11 full-time book-keepers just to keep up with the bureaucracy of the taxation system.

Impact

In the first year TCK worked with a strong church in Almaty and we saw the people in our programme grow and change, get water baptized, baptized in the Holy Spirit and move on in their relationship with God. By the end of the second year the first church – called 'Freedom' – was planted. This generated some disquiet as five of the seven deacons were ex-heroin addicts and all of them contributed to the preaching.

The local Christian community has been powerfully impacted by the incredible miracles God has done in relation to this work. There are no long-term sponsors other than Tearfund UK, so God has had to do many miracles just to keep everyone alive. Also, because TCK deals with drug addiction, the discipline is far greater than in a non-residential community, so it has been able to organize many things that other churches would be unable to do because the people are more reliable and obedient.

Evaluation

When the programme began, people were only asked to pay what they could afford, but this was abused with people paying nothing at all. We realized that the people had a different attitude towards money as a result of communism. They saw a rich foreign organization that could support them just as the welfare system had done. Families are now means-tested and are required to declare all their income and assets.

We have learned that there will always be people who criticize you – not just from the world, but also from the church. But we cannot allow such criticism to turn us from obedience to God.

On the positive side we have learned many good points. First, that with God all things are possible and there is always an anointing for work with the poor. Second, you must have strong leadership. The spiritual life of the leader is the most important issue. Third, nothing grows quickly. And finally, if you keep working, God will keep building.

Financing the work and training workers are the greatest challenges. Some of the best workers in other countries are those who have graduated from the programme and this is proving to be the case in Kazakstan as well. TCK relies on the community for its operational costs. Since we began in 1995 we have operated as a commune, paying small salaries and relying on donations to help feed our students and workers. We have experienced great hardship, but God has kept us. Lack of funds and workers have been overcome by faith, prayer and fasting. Despite these problems the programme has doubled every year since the beginning.

Part Three

Integral Mission and the Church

Integral Mission and the Church

Archbishop Donald Mtetemala

In my work as the bishop of a small diocese in Tanzania I
visit each parish at least once a year. This gives me the
opportunity to talk about the needs of the community and
the response of the church to those needs with members of
the church and community leaders. The diocese has
become more active in responding to the physical needs of
the poor communities because we saw this as a way of
bringing God's love among them. Evangelism has always
remained central to our mission, but the more we do
evangelism, the more God shows us the broadness of his
mission. We are learning that mission must not be narrow,
because it is God's mission. The church's mission
originates from God's mission and as such it must be
broad enough to touch both the soul and the body, the
society as well as the individual. It must have an impact on
people in their *total* need. It must be integral, total and
wholesome.

It is not that this is a new thing to us. We have heard
about it and have read statements on the need for the
church to see its mission as integral and not fall into the

error of presenting mission in a narrow sense, emphasizing either the spiritual or physical alone. The problem, however, has always been 'to make those statements live'; to 'put the statements into action'. In my diocese we have defined our mission as being 'to empower the marginalized groups to identify and address their physical and spiritual problems'. Our vision is 'to have empowered community living life in its fullness'.

During the last ten years we have seen ourselves compelled to take the whole gospel to the whole person. It has given us much joy to bring God's love to his people by offering water services, community health programmes, food for the hungry, educational services, agricultural education and above all the privilege of bringing good news about the saving work of Jesus Christ for all sinners. We have not just seen people benefit from material blessings, but have seen them receive with joy the forgiveness and love of Jesus Christ.

I have given this background so that you can see where I come from and what my work as a bishop involves. This paper considers the future of integral mission for the poor and the church. The subject addresses the importance of impact in our mission. We all agree on the importance of putting emphasis on integral mission. The problem is making those words – our statements and resolutions – become flesh. The people we represent here will not benefit from resolutions alone. The poor have heard and read many resolutions that at first sparked hope, but later that hope faded away. It is when we become doers of what we resolve that we shall begin seeing some impact in the life of the people we are called to serve.

The country from which I come contains poor communities characterized by low income, malnutrition, ill health, illiteracy, insecurity, helplessness and isolation. Development agencies have analysed the causes of poverty among such individuals and communities in poor countries like mine. The causes include human exploitation, selfish greed, oppression, lack of justice, disease, illiteracy, lack of technical know-how, national income mismanagement and so on. As a leader of the church I ask myself how we as a church can respond effectively to the needs of such poor people.

I have seen mission agencies and non-mission agencies work to fight poverty. I have seen Christian groups advocating for the poor before various governments. Yet, as I look at my own situation, I sense that we still have a long way to go to have an impact among the poor. It is therefore important to think through our future direction as agencies and churches devoted to doing God's mission.

1. The Centrality of God and the Gospel

If the church is called by grace to be involved in the mission of God, then it must hold the gospel central in its mission. This will differentiate the mission of God and that of the world. Our mission flows from God's mission. God's mission is manifested to the church through the life, work and death of Jesus Christ. God sends the Son. The Son sends the Holy Spirit. And the Son sends out the church into the world: 'As the Father has sent me, I am sending you' (Jn. 20:21).

The further we drift away from God, the more we lose sight of God's mission. We cannot claim to do God's mission if God is not at the centre of the mission we seek to do. Scripture, too, must be central in our understanding of mission. We study Scripture to learn what his will is in his mission. Drifting away from Scripture is dangerous.

We have therefore to be continuously reminded about the message that we are called to take to the world. The message is Jesus Christ himself. He is the gospel – the good news to the world. As such, he is our motif for mission. We are motivated to take God's love to the world because of what God did in Christ on the cross. This makes the cross central to our mission. If we lose sight of Jesus then we lose sight of God's mission, because Jesus was doing his Father's business.

Jesus, therefore, must be central to our mission. From him we shall learn what God's will is as we engage in his mission. The future of integral mission depends on how faithful the church remains as a steward of the gospel of Christ. The gospel is one essential foundation stone in our integral mission because the church has been entrusted with the gospel that brings peace to the whole person. It is a gospel of God's love that permeates every sphere of human need and responds positively to the whole person both in his or her physical and spiritual hunger.

2. Moving Beyond a Traditional Understanding of Mission

Our understanding of mission today has changed a lot from the traditional understanding of mission. Traditionally there were mission fields and non-mission fields. Today we live in a world that cannot be divided into Christian and non-Christian fields. Today we witness religiously pluralistic societies where non-Christian faiths rub shoulders with the Christian faith. All this forces us to think afresh what mission is. It is no longer the sending of 'missionaries' across the seas, for we are now realizing that the mission field is on our doorstep!

The advancement of modern technology means that today we know more of the situation in the world. We analyse better the causes of poverty because the tools for such exercises are more advanced. This helps us to see economic imbalance in the world – how the rich get richer and the poor get poorer. All this broadens our understanding of mission.

The advancement of modern technology and science, however, has also brought with it the winds of secularization. People have become nominal in their faith. The Christian countries from which mission enterprises originated, or from which they were spearheaded, are not immune from this secularization. Mission cannot mean the same thing even for them.

We know better today that God is involved in the whole world – not just meeting the spiritual needs of some continents, but responding to the whole world. We are learning that the Christian faith must not be kept within ourselves, but that we must express it in the world where God has placed us. We are learning that mission must be the concern of every individual Christian. Mission is the way that Christians express their faith. This is not just for Western countries, but even for those countries that were once termed 'mission fields'. The whole world is to be seen as mission field – not just 'over there'. Whether people are materially rich or poor, they all need to realize who God is in their lives so that they can see their place in the world and what God's will is for them. We are learning that just as we take the witness of the gospel seriously, so we must take seriously how we are to express in a practical way the faith we have found in Jesus. We are learning that the good news must impact both on the spiritual and the physical if it is to bring life abundant in its fullness (see Jn. 10:10).

In short we are learning that mission is not just baptizing people as Christians, but *helping the baptized to see how they can serve Christ in the world in which they live.*

3. The Centrality of the Local Church

Let us consider the responsibility of the church for reaching out to the world with the gospel of love. The church here is that 'body of the faithful' who have believed in Jesus Christ and acknowledge him as their Lord. These churches are there in our communities. God has by grace chosen to involve these churches in his mission.

We as development and Christian agencies cannot avoid the local church as we seek to bring love to the poor. It will be through this local church that we shall be able to move into the community. It is true that there have been times when the local church has neglected her responsibility to take God's love to the world. This has encouraged the creation of Christian agencies and mission societies to fulfil this neglected mission of the local church. Our role, however, is not to replace local churches, but to build their capacity and remind them of their calling to take God's love to the communities around them.

As members within the local church discover their gifts and apply them in service for Christ, the community will be the place where they will go out to fulfil God's mission. Local churches must understand their place in the community as well as the broadness of God's mission. They must understand how integral God's mission is. Then they will have the privilege of manifesting God's love to their communities in an integrated way rather than just focusing on spiritual needs. This is one way of being salt in the community.

In my diocese we have a parish called St Luke's. We challenged them to start a day feeding centre for street children. They did not understand why as a church they had to be involved in this community work. It took a long time for many of them to realize how they can show their love for Christ by reaching out to those in physical need. The feeding centre is still there and stands as a reminder to the Christians that their mission must be integral if it is to bring meaning to the people around them.

The future of integral mission must therefore be in the enabling of local churches so that they can serve as instruments to transform the communities around them. This is not to emphasize building up the institutional church; rather *it is transforming local churches so they realize their mission in the world*.

4. Making Integral Mission Central in our Ecumenical Dialogues

Three years ago I attended a consultation in South Africa that brought together representatives of the Lutheran church and the Anglican church in Africa. We spent time trying to discover our common ground and the concerns we faced as churches. This gave us a good basis to see how we could begin to relate as we do God's mission. We realized that often Christians at grass-roots level wrestle together to fight common issues. At the grass roots they do not work in their denominational groupings – they work together as one church. The representatives decided to highlight those common issues so that we could see how to work out a common strategy to solve those issues. We cited the problems of poverty, HIV/AIDS, suffering from civil wars, political unrest, refugees, fundament- alism, corruption and social injustices. This gave us a reason to continue working together.

This is what I mean when I talk about making mission central in our ecumenical dialogues. Sometimes we spend so much time trying to agree on 'a particular theology'. Although this may be important, the danger is that we may forget in our dialogues why God sends us out as 'churches' into the world. Ecumenical dialogues have a key role in enhancing integral mission through our local churches.

5. Focusing on the Community rather than on the Church

Sometimes we invest money and resources in developing the institutional church. We have laboured to improve the image of the church or even the image of our denominations. This is a temptation all of us face. This has even made us labour hard to fill our church buildings regardless of the depth of faith people may have. This gives us a narrow concept of mission. Some development agencies have fallen into the same problem. They have laboured to build the image of their organization rather than that of the community.

As a church, if we are to do God's mission, then we must see our role as being *in the world*. What is the place of our local church in the community that surrounds it? To where is Jesus sending us? To where does the word 'Go' lead us?

In Tanzania we have what we call mission stations where our mission workers (or 'missionaries') live. They are green islands that have every essential need for those who live there. Often, however, the communities that surround them are very poor and what goes on at the mission station has no impact on them. The mission station belongs to the church and the church's image is good to the extent that the mission station serves as a demonstration centre. But if it fails to make an impact on the community then it has failed in its mission.

Churches must have the community as a priority for their mission. There in the community they have the opportunity to put into practice God's love. That is where poverty, sickness and ignorance prevail. If integral mission is to have a lasting effect it must be demonstrated in the community. Communities, with their different faces and different needs, must be the focus of our mission. Our efforts must not only be to build the church into a strong institution for its own sake! We need to make the church a servant in the society in which it bears witness.

6. Focusing on the Poor in our Communities

Someone once said if you removed all the references to the poor from the pages of the Bible you may end up having no Bible at all. God's concern for the poor is central in Scripture.

> Do not deny justice to your poor people in their lawsuits (Ex. 23:6).

> However, there should be no poor among you, for in the land the Lord your God is giving you to possess as your inheritance, he will richly bless you … (Deut. 15:4).

> They trample on the heads of the poor as upon the dust of the ground and deny justice to the oppressed (Amos 2:7).

> You trample on the poor and force him to give you grain. Therefore, though you have built stone mansions, you will not live in them; though you have planted lush vineyards, you will not drink their wine (Amos 5:11).

> But you have insulted the poor. Is it not the rich who are exploiting you? Are they not the ones who are dragging you into court? (Jas. 2:6).

The church, therefore, cannot ignore the poor. It must have a concern for the poor and make them central in its mission agenda. 'You will always have the poor among you,' Jesus once remarked (Jn. 12:8). We witness poverty in its lowest ebb. We see people dying because of poverty. The church has a role to play to alleviate this pain caused by poverty and it can only do so if the poor are a target for its mission. After all, who is not poor? Are we all spiritually, economically, socially and politically rich? Do we have life abundant in all these areas of life?

To hold the poor central in our mission we need to have God's heart. We must be motivated by him to render service to the poor. God himself must move our hearts (see Jas. 5:11; Lk. 6:36).

7. Working in Collaboration with other Development Agencies

It is important to bear in mind that we as Christians cannot work in isolation. We share some common goals with non-Christian agencies and we need, therefore, to find ways of working together. We need to learn how others involve the poor in bringing change into their lives. Learning from other development agencies will help us to identify pitfalls to avoid as we involve the poor in this long journey of alleviating poverty. We need to collaborate as we work together for the common goal of fighting poverty.

It is most important, however, that as we collaborate with other agencies we do not lose sight of Jesus, the motive of our mission. Since our mission is God's mission, we must always remember that we offer something far above the material well-being of a person.

Finally, you need to be a prophet to tell the future of integral mission. I believe, however, that the most important thing for all the stakeholders of mission is to see God as central to their understanding and definition of mission. To lose Christ is to lose the focus of our mission.

'As the Father has sent me, I am sending you' (Jn. 20:21).

Integral Mission in a World of Violence

Peter Kuzmič

International politics has been preoccupied in the last decade with the task of managing conflict, specifically interethnic conflict. We have recently witnessed violence and brutality in Kosovo and East Timor, despite the fact that the international community in these places intervened at an earlier stage than in Rwanda and Bosnia. In 1999 there were 29 interethnic conflicts in the world and there are a dozen places in the world where new ethnic violence could break out. According to the United Nations High Commissioner for Refugees, between 1991 and 1995 the number of refugees in our world increased from 17 million to 27 million. When you talk to refugees you discover what human dramas these people bring. How to manage international and interethnic conflicts will remain a major task of the international community. For the last nine years we in the Balkans have lived on a war-driven roller coaster after the communist ideology was replaced by conflicting nationalistic ideologies. As Leon Trotsky said in a different context, if anyone longs for a quiet lifestyle, they have certainly chosen the wrong epoch to live in. As Christians we are asking the question: How is the believing community to respond?

A Christian Perspective on Conflict

The last century had more soldiers and civilians killed in wars than the previous 5,000 years of recorded history, and four times as many as in the previous four centuries cumulatively. But why so many wars and victims in just one century? Theories abound, yet many are deficient from a Christian perspective for they fail to address the deepest ambiguities of human nature and that funda-mental alienation of human beings from their Creator that results in their alienation from each other. Over 112 million people (some estimates go much higher) were killed in what at its outset was expected to be the 'century of elevated human reason'. As Reinhold Niebuhr said, the Christian doctrine of sin is the least popular doctrine, and yet the one for which we have the most overwhelming empirical evidence everywhere.

Samuel Huntington, in his book *The Clash of Civilizations*, highlights the role of religion in shaping new kinds of warfare driven primarily not by issues of economics or territory, but by clashes of different ideologies and civilizations.[60] But while the international diplomats are discovering the destructive role of religion, they also

---

[60] Samuel P Huntington, *The Clash of Civilizations and the Remaking of the World Order* (New York: Simon & Schuster, 1996). For a more Christian and constructive approach see Douglas Johnston and Cynthia Sampson (eds), *Religion, the Missing Dimension of Statecraft* (New York/Oxford: OUP, 1994); Miroslav Volf, *Exclusion and Embrace: A Theological*

discover that religion has a great potential for social healing, for forgiveness, for reconciliation, for building bridges of understanding and confidence across ethnic and other divides. Frequently modern conflicts are explained as 'normal' reactions to the processes of globalization. Small ethnic communities and their cultures feel threatened by the aggressive forces of globalization as they invade their territories.

Kenneth Waltz offers three explanations for the origins of wars in Western history.[61] One is what he calls *folly of the nations*. Nation states are organized to pursue wars, whether the wars are due to the economic self-interest, national pride, national insecurity or the political pressure of the masses or sometimes the military or the political leaders. A second explanation is *international anarchy* or *disorder*. Waltz says that as long as there is no ruler to enforce order, autonomous units of the international system will resort to armed conflict to resolve their tensions. These tensions may be due to economic competition, exaggerated nationalism, border disputes, territorial claims or ideological clashes, but it is international anarchy that permits wars. But Waltz looks at yet a third explanation. He speaks not only of the folly of the nations, but of flawed *human nature*. This of course is a euphemistic reference to what we Christians call sin, a recognition that humans are flawed. This weakness of persons is due to the fundamental alienation from our Creator, who is a God of peace. Whether the major cause

---

[60] (continued) *Exploration of Identity, Otherness, and Reconciliation* (Nashville, Tennessee: Abingdon, 1996); and Donald W Shriver, *An Ethic for Enemies: Forgiveness in Politics* (New York: Oxford University Press, 1998).

[61] See Kenneth N Waltz, *Man, the State and War: A Theoretical Analysis* (New York: Columbia University Press, 1959, 2001).

be ignorance, pride, greed or social estrangement, the problem lies in human nature.

The problem with a Marxist approach is not only its problematic use of class struggle and violence but also its optimistic anthropology. Marxism has an optimistic view of human beings that is marked by theoretical absence of sin. This is why it is important for Christians to bring the perspective of the kingdom of God. Alexander Solzhenitsyn said that the twentieth century was ending as the most cannibalistic century of all. I think that we have a unique opportunity as Christian theologians and missiologists to bring a perspective on the present reality that has been lacking. A Christian perspective illuminates this tragedy of human beings' reliance on their pride and their selfish search for power. They do not submit to the Lord of the nations, but rather submit in their vanity to work out their own destiny and to decide the fate of their nations. Dethroning God inevitably leads to human tragedy.

A Christian Response to Interethnic Violence

Let us briefly look at Bosnia as a case study of a Christian response to interethnic violence.

The ancient boundary between east and west runs through former Yugoslavia whose complex make-up included six republics and two autonomous regions, five Slavic nationalities along with several strong national minorities, two alphabets and three main religions (Orthodox, Roman Catholicism and Islam). Misha Glenny called Bosnia–Herzegovina 'the paradise of the damned'.[62]

---

[62] Misha Glenny, *The Fall of Yugoslavia* (London: Penguin, 1992), chapter 5.

There were three myths about the war in Bosnia. One was that it was primarily an ethnic or tribal conflict due to an uncontrollable eruption of ancient ethnic hatreds. This explanation, however, fails when faced with the fact that every third marriage in Bosnian cities was interethnic and that there was a peaceful coexistence between ethno-religious communities for centuries. The second myth was that in Bosnia we had a classical civil war. In reality, it was an imported war, engineered and supported by Belgrade and shaped by their expansionist concept of 'Greater Serbia'. The third myth speaks of 'the defence of the Christian West against the onslaught of fundamentalist Islam' in Europe. But for most Bosnians Islam is more of an issue of cultural identity than a religious designation. Many Bosnian Muslims are atheists or religious agnostics and it is certainly inaccurate to describe them as 'militant fundamentalists' threatening 'Christian Europe'. The genesis of the war was ideological and territorial, not ethnic or religious. Political leaders with ambitions to enlarge their territories regardless of the human cost manipulated ethnic and religious sentiments. It was in their interest to create the perception that it was an inevitable ethno-religious war and they were able to create it by the manipulation of media, over which they had almost total control.

When the war began, the international community imposed an arms embargo on the whole of Yugoslavia. Serbian generals controlling the old Yugoslav Army had a monopoly on arms and thus a distinct military advantage over the republics. They staged an aggressive war in strategic alliance with the communist oligarchy still ruling in Belgrade. Pro-democratically oriented Slovenes, Croats and Bosnians became victims who initially had no arms to defend themselves while the Belgrade aggressors armed the Serbian minorities. This explains why one-third of Croatia was occupied in a short time, as was 70 per cent of Bosnia–Herzegovina, leaving 200,000 dead and about 3 million as refugees.

How do you respond to a situation like that as a Christian? Allow me to share a personal story. I had evacuated my family from the city of Osijek, although not in time to prevent my daughter being traumatized for years by what she experienced during the intensive bombing. We had also evacuated the seminary, of which I was the director. Now I sat in my office at Gordon-Conwell Theological Seminary, Boston, Massachusetts, working on a book in a safe and peaceful environment. As I was writing one day the phone rang. It was Dr Kramaric, the major of Osijek. The city was under severe bombardment. Every third house had been hit. Out of a population of 125,000 only 19,000 people were left. Nearby Vukovar was totally destroyed and some hospitals in the area were about to start operating without anaesthetic. Dr Kramaric said: 'You are a Christian and as a Christian, you cannot be indifferent.' Suddenly I pushed my manuscript aside because I noticed tears falling down my cheeks as I came under the conviction that I was involved in a selfish academic exercise of promoting my own career while priority should be given to saving lives.

I travelled back, entering Osijek on a small, dangerous road, along with several of my formers students who were now themselves refugees. We discovered there was no food and no medical assistance. When my hands touched a limbless boy in the basement of the bombed-out hospital something revolutionary started taking place in both my heart and my mind. I almost dare to say that my theology changed.

Risking our lives for the second time, my friends and I went back to Zagreb in search of food and medical assistance. I went to visit an old friend, a Catholic priest who was a good friend of Protestant evangelicals and a man with a great heart. We both cried as Father Jurak told me that he had 7,000 people to feed with only a day's food for 200. Despite three days without sleep, I spent the night calling people around the world. 'If you believe in God,' I pleaded with them, 'please send us some food, do something about it.'

With some of our evangelical ministers we founded a relief agency called Agape. It would be a two-hands ministry: with one hand we would give daily bread because people were physically hungry; with the other hand we would offer the eternal bread because they were spiritually hungry. Just a few months later war would break out in Bosnia and we would have the opportunity to help thousands of lives there and many more during the Kosovo crisis.

What have we learned about responding to pain and suffering through interethnic violence in the Balkans? Let me briefly answer that question by outlining the three Cs of integral mission.

1. Context

Evangelicals emphasize the text of God's word, the Bible, as authoritative for belief and practice. Ministers of the gospel must be competent interpreters of Scripture. The text is, however, neither proclaimed nor practised in a vacuum but always in a concrete situation or context. All of Christian life and mission is a two-way street with constant traffic between the text and the context, between God's holy word and God's alienated world. If we ignore the world, we betray the word because the word sends us into the world. If we ignore the word, like some of our liberal friends, we will have nothing to bring to the world.

People need a message of hope and life for situations of despair and death. We have learned that there is no authentic mission from a safe distance. Mission with integrity does not take place in antiseptic conditions.

I have frequently struggled with the question of how to evangelize in painful situations without appearing to exploit human suffering. Entering the context is of crucial importance. Jesus did not pick up a heavenly megaphone to shout down to the inhabitants of Planet Earth: 'Repent!' He entered human history and human flesh. He was hungry. He was thirsty. He became a refugee. Contextualization is not just knowledge of the other context, but being willing to identify yourself with the context and become vulnerable.

One of our American missionary educators in Osijek Seminary, Chris Marshall, had been involved in a small traffic accident and was left in hospital when we evacuated. After her release she decided to stay in the basement of our seminary taking care of the elderly and wounded and caring for our Serbian neighbours whom we were sheltering from possible Croatian revenge. Despite being the only American left in Croatia, she refused to leave. When confronted with the order of her government she calmly responded: 'I have higher orders to obey.' She stayed throughout the war and became known in the city as the 'Evangelical Mother Theresa of Osijek'. Integral mission is always incarnationally contextual.

2. Compassion

We evangelicals know about the Great Commission (Mt. 28:19). But we must read it in the context of Christ's claim to have been given all power and authority (Mt. 28:18).

Jesus can legitimately make that claim because he is the only one who walked this earth whose hands never stole, whose lips never lied, whose heart was without any wrong motive and in whose mind there was no erroneous thought. Although fully human, he was the only one without sin, which uniquely qualified him to take the sins of humanity to the cross. And he is the only one who came back from death. This event and his supreme authority are the theological bases for the evangelizing task: 'Therefore go and make disciples of all nations.'

We, as 'Great Commission Christians', discovered in the basements of Croatia and Bosnia Matthew 25. Jesus says the results of the final accounting day will depend on how we treated the hungry, the thirsty, the naked, the refugees and the prisoners. Matthew 25 is the Great Compassion Chapter while Matthew 28 is the Great Commission Chapter. Both are the words of our Lord and we must keep them together if we are to be authentic witnesses for Christ in the painful situations of our broken world.

We have learned that proclamation alone in such situations can be counterproductive because it smacks of religious propaganda and senseless proselytizing. People do not only have souls that we register for heaven; they also have bodies that need to be taken care of. They have not only ears to hear what we say; they also have eyes to observe whether we truly live according to what we proclaim. There is no authentic mission without the motivation of love and the practice of compassion. Indifference to suffering and injustice is sin. George Bernard Shaw once said that the worst sin towards our fellow creatures is not to hate them, but to be indifferent to them. This is the essence of inhumanity. A letter in *Time* magazine made the same point: that death in Rwanda in harrowing proportions came not only from massacres and cholera, but also from apathy. Jesus, we are told, saw the crowds and was moved with compassion (Mt. 9:36). He loved them to the point of pain. Having the eyes and heart of Jesus is a key to integral mission. Vision and love are basic preconditions for any missionary work.

3. Credibility

In one of our Lausanne congresses we met under the slogan: 'How Shall They Hear?' There was a serious polar- ization between Third World evangelicals and Western, especially North American, evangelicals. The latter emphasized the priority of evangelism in the sense of the verbalization of the message of salvation. Some of us living at that time under Marxism or in other antagonistic contexts of our broken world said 'How shall they hear?' is a biblical question because it is taken from Romans 10, but it is not fully biblical because in many places of the world the first question is not 'How shall they hear?' but 'What shall they see?' What they see will determine their response to what they hear.

Money, management and methods are not sufficient for evangelism. A purely managerial approach to mission is a secular, consumerist, pragmatic and unbiblical view. In many places of the world the Christian church must regain its credibility because it has been so compromised. When taking theological students on pioneering mission trips in former communist Yugoslavia I would often tell them that our first task may be simply to wash the face of Jesus because it had been distorted and dirtied by the compromises of institutional Christianity through the centuries and through Marxist atheistic propaganda in more recent times. We have a credible message of a credible Saviour, but the more difficult question is whether we have credible communities and credible messengers.

At the end of the war in Bosnia I met with the Muslim mayor of the city of Bihac. Bihac was cut off from the rest of the world for over three years. Over one thousand children lost at least one parent as a result of indiscriminate shelling. The hospital operated without anaesthetic for months. Some of Agape's volunteers risked their lives to help and now Agape was to be honoured 'for saving lives'. During our pleasant visit I asked the mayor, 'You are a Muslim and I am a Christian. How is it that we get along this well?' He smiled and said:

> That's because I am not the kind of Muslim your friends from the West think about when they hear the word Muslim, and you are not the kind of Christian that Muslims think about when we hear the word Christian. I have a Muslim name; I am culturally Muslim; but I am not really a devout follower of Islam. I don't have a deep commitment to Allah but I am increasingly interested in Jesus because of who you people are and what you do. You are not the kind of Christians that fit our mental image and prejudice, because you have not come for territorial gains or with a political agenda or ethnic exclusivity. You did not come like the crusaders with the sword in one hand and the cross in the other. Instead, you have loved us without pushing your religion down our throats.

Then he added that we were free to open a church in his city because they trusted us. When I asked why they trusted us he simply responded:

> You are credible with us because you became vulnerable with us.

Credibility depends on our availability, which includes our vulnerability. The mayor's comment gave me a wonderful opportunity to share with him the story of the most credible person that ever walked the earth. Jesus is the most credible person because he became vulnerable by his incarnation and the Cross. He is our model missionary whose gospel we are to live, proclaim and practise with contextual sensitivity, compassionate engagement and credible witness. That is what integral mission is all about

Case Study

Conflict and Relief:
the Evangelical Church of Guinea-Bissau

Tiago Sampaio

Overview

Organization
The Evangelical Church of Guinea-Bissau (Igreja
Evangelica da Guine-Bissau)

Project description
Relief through the local church in the context of civil war

Issues
Relief, conflict, mobilizing the church, integral mission

Context

There is high ethnic diversity among the communities and the 23 different ethnic groups with whom the Evangelical Church of Guinea-Bissau (IEGB) works. Some of these social groupings are organized along vertical lines, their members more often than not being Islamic and grouped around a chief whom all respect. Others are organized on horizontal lines and are essentially animistic. They do not have a traditional chief although the older members of such societies are generally respected and have the last word in decision making. In both types of society there is a high rate of illiteracy, and sanitation, access to clean water and educational services are usually inadequate. Despite this, the people are hospitable and friendly. They have a fatalistic attitude to their poverty.

There are significant cultural differences among the ethnic groups, but there are also common cultural traits arising from a long history of close social contact between the societies in question. Such common cultural areas include circumcision, marriage and funeral rites, a common trade language and a shared experience of being colonized by the Portuguese. Around 80 per cent of the population are farmers whose livelihoods are based on agriculture and cattle rearing. Their income is limited, which explains both the low national economic productivity and the migration – especially of the youth – towards urban centres to chase their dreams of a better life.

The level of poverty is high. Guinea-Bissau is ranked 162nd out of the 175 nations listed in the human development index.[63] The essential causes of this poverty appear to be ignorance, spiritual blindness and conformism.

---

[63] United Nations Development Programme (UNDP), *Human Development Report 2000*.

The religious practices of the majority of the population are broadly animist, with Islam in second place. By comparison, membership of IEGB is a little over 1 per cent of the population.

Description

The aim of the work of IEGB was to alleviate the suffering of the people by responding to both their physical and spiritual needs. Then without warning civil war broke out in June 1998. The people were panic-stricken by a political and military conflict lasting 11 months, which included incidents of a nature unprecedented in their history. People were scattered widely across the country. The task of IEGB became reaching out to refugees in a two-stage programme – first to those within a 20-kilometre radius of the capital city, Bissau, and later to those more widely spread across the country. We wanted to arrange for the supply of food, water and sanitation to the tens of thousands of people in need as well as to bring them words of moral sustenance and comfort. IEGB was approached by many people asking for help. The Minister of Health asked if we could do something and the World Food Programme accepted IEGB to support the displaced population. The violence of the conflict had resulted in the population seeking refuge not only within the country itself but also abroad in Gambia, Senegal, Guinea, the Cape Verde Islands and Portugal, where the same range of assistance was required.

Results

The effect of IEGB's work was rapidly and widely felt thanks to its centralized organization and to the work of local churches. The local churches played a vital role. Because pastors knew their communities, it was easier to target assistance on the most needy. Social projects were maintained throughout the conflict, enabling the work undertaken by the Department of Social Action and Development of IEGB in areas such as drinking water, medical assistance, assistance to prisoners of war, agricultural production and education to be continued. The project owes its success to the logistic organization so rapidly put in place by the church and to the collective will to serve displayed by its members.

Impact

As a result of its response to the conflict, the IEGB not only gained credibility in the eyes of its partner institutions, but earned a place of honour in the minds of the population, including the Islamic community. The credibility and acceptance of the church by the wider community significantly increased during the conflict. The communities affected by the conflict received the help they needed – both materially and spiritually – and the church has grown in numbers and spiritual health. Several families have been reunited with their local church having accepted the challenge of the Christian life. Despite the impact of the war, the church's development work is going better than before. IEGB took on the challenge of responding to communities affected by war and was thereby able to demonstrate its ability to mobilize itself to the service of others.

On both a local and central level, the local church communities have put into practice their sense of social responsibility. They are now better prepared to deal with future challenges while concentrating their present efforts, both material and spiritual, on ensuring that such conflict does not arise in future. The social action undertaken by local churches has had the effect of pulling people together to face other social situations.

Evaluation

The experience we have gained has shown us that the risks we took – even that of loss of life – were worthwhile. All of us who took part in the programmes found our lives enriched by the diverse experiences we lived through. At the same time, we are agreed that we should invest our energy in preventing a repetition of war in our country.

Inevitably, the war had a devastating impact, but this did not deviate project workers from carrying out their objectives. Often the impact of the war was overcome by the exemplary influence of project workers. Christians were made aware of the need to combine faith with practical service on a daily basis. They were able to experience at first hand how faith without service is meaningless and how service reinforces faith: Love the Lord your God – and your brothers and sisters.

Case Study

Church-Based Rural Development: RDIS, Rwanda

John Wesley Kabango

Overview

Organization
Rural Development Interdiocesan Service (RDIS), Episcopal Church of Rwanda

Project description
Church-based integrated rural development

Issues
Mobilizing the church, rural development, reconciliation, integral mission

Context

The 1994 genocide in Rwanda left the government, the church and the international community with a number of formidable challenges. With nearly a million people killed in the space of three months, the social fabric of the country was destroyed, the economy left in ruins, and natural and human resources seriously depleted. The genocide decimated the professional and educated classes. Rwanda was already one of the world's poorest countries before the genocide and the events of 1994 led to a catastrophic increase in poverty, with 70 per cent of households below the poverty line. Many women are heading households because their husbands were killed or are in prison.

An estimated 130,000 detainees accused of genocide are incarcerated in overcrowded prisons. The government and the judicial system have been concerned by this problem and a participatory justice process is being organized whereby the detainees are going to be taken to their villages to be judged by the community members.

More than 90 per cent of the population, obliged to cultivate shrinking plots of land of declining quality, is dependent on agriculture for existence. Yet the agricultural sector is constrained by structural problems: declining soil productivity; low use of appropriate inputs; and excessive state intervention in favour of cash crops (coffee and tea). One serious problem in the aftermath of the genocide is the shortage of farming labour. Moreover, in the past few years, Rwanda has suffered from poor harvests provoked by El Niño.

Life expectancy is 48 years compared with an average of 54 years in sub-Saharan Africa. Infant mortality is 125 per 1,000 births. One in every four infants is malnourished.

Eleven per cent of the rural population and twelve per cent of the urban population is thought to be HIV positive. The infection of 12- to 14-year-olds has increased sharply.

Less than 50 per cent of the population has access to safe water. Most of the water systems, including water catchment areas, were either destroyed or deteriorated during the war and genocide.

There have been serious contradictions in the positions of both the Roman Catholic and Protestant churches in Rwanda. The moral authority of the Christian religion has been systematically undermined by the readiness of some leaders to make accommodations with the powers that prepared the genocide. There is a strong feeling across the country that the church must be reborn. Rwanda, the church included, has adopted a culture of not admitting the wrongdoing and mistakes of the past, of the present or, I fear, of the future. The church in Rwanda has fallen victim to a culture of silence and fear.

In many churches there is an urgent need to create a broader awareness of justice, peace and the integrity of creation. Integral mission is seen as alien to common religious practice and is left to a few individuals. There is a lack of a biblical explanation of the relationship between development and faith. Many church leaders do not recognize that justice involves overcoming exclusion and enhancing participation.

Description

RDIS owes its existence to the desire of the four dioceses of the Episcopal Church in Rwanda (Butare, Cyangugu, Kigeme and Shyogwe) to work for the development of the poorest of the poor. Activities include evangelism, teaching on forgiveness and reconciliation, animal husbandry, food production, micro-enterprise development, fisheries, bee-keeping and tree nurseries.

The vision of RDIS is 'a holy soul in a healthy body' with a focus on the person as a whole. We believe that people oppressed by economic, social and political systems should appeal to God to intervene in order that their rights be restored (Ps. 146:7–9). God's justice concerns social relationships and aims at creating an egalitarian community in which the basic needs of all classes of people are met. RDIS believes that committed Christians with the ability to access basic needs will sustain the church's activities. It is our conviction that the church holds the key to the real development of life in Rwanda and that God is longing to use its ministry to transform the physical, spiritual and social lives of ordinary people and the environment in which they live.

RDIS was set up to help the church use its land to build the spiritual and material life of rural communities. Church land is not simply an opportunity to earn money, but more importantly a God-given place to meet ordinary people, understand their needs, care for their immediate needs and show that Jesus Christ has the answer to their deepest needs.

Christian development does not mean organizations, buildings or projects, but building up mature Christians and teaching them skills to improve the quality of their lives and communities. We have encouraged participatory processes to take place with the aim of implementing projects that reflect as much as possible the involvement and participation of the community at the grass roots.

RDIS operates through church structures and the church has been instrumental in enabling RDIS to achieve its objective. It has provided office accommodation and land to establish demonstration centres and venues for meetings and training. Pastors and catechists have provided advice, fostered holistic ministry through their preaching and daily activities, promoted outreach to vulnerable groups and supported the work through fellowship and prayer. And some have become development animators trained by RDIS.

Results

Development activities such as farming associations provide a context for evangelism and reconciliation. There is a need to extend this work to embrace the entire community, addressing the needs of the poorest of the poor. The animators and the group leaders currently lack reconciliation and counselling skills to enable them address peace-building issues and handle trauma cases in the groups. RDIS is encouraging and facilitating the process of group formation through training sessions.

RDIS is attempting to increase food production at household level. Nearly 6,000 families have benefited from the demonstration centres that have been established in the dioceses. These have encouraged food security through the introduction of non-traditional hunger crops, drought crops and quick nature crops.

Since 1994 there has been massive destruction of trees for firewood and construction, which threatens to have a long-term impact on the environment and contribute to the prolonged drought. In response RDIS has established seven nursery beds in the four dioceses.

Impact

The meetings of the farming associations provide an opportunity for praying, praising and sharing faith in addition to being together as a family. Many assisted groups show indications of unity, ethnic mix, integration and a shared focus on improving their lives. The emphasis on spiritual revival has enhanced awareness among the members of their situation and the need to put all their problems before God.

Evangelism and reconciliation interventions have provided an opportunity for the community members to meet and build trust. Acts of compassion to the vulnerable are evident in the groups. RDIS witnesses groups of people making bricks to build a house for the homeless, widows or orphans. Contributions for medical bills, food for the vulnerable and sharing of seeds can be seen in many groups. And there is evidence of increased participation in church activities.

Evaluation

The churches in Rwanda need to sharpen their commitment to caring for and comforting individuals and families as our loved ones. Families are torn apart and marriages are failing. I believe that healthy families will produce healthy societies. The task of the Christians will be to find ways to heal this brokenness around us. Our church leaders will require refresher courses to help them stand at the forefront of the new struggle facing churches today. They will need to read the signs of the times and interpret them to the churches, to society and to those in authority. Christian values and the prophetic voices of the churches were not stilled in the past. They must remain strong in the future if the churches are to contribute to genuine integral mission.

Christians often see peace as calm and tranquillity. But peace is the fruit of justice. The biblical concept of shalom involves right relationships among people, communities and nations. It is founded on the God of reconciliation. My experience is that reconciliation starts when conflicting parties are ready to be reconciled with God. Only as we experience forgiveness are we able to forgive. It is in this framework that justice is restored.

Let us walk in the light of God in obedience to the gospel of Jesus Christ. This implies that we as the church:

- shall have courage to persuade people
- shall present ourselves fearlessly before people so they develop pride and respect in us
- shall be compelled by Christ's love
- shall allow the process of renewal and prophetic obedience to God
- shall have creative love that controls life
- shall be prepared to renounce popularity for the sake of the risen Christ
- shall develop a long-term, millennium vision, leading to a joint, united ministry focusing on eternity
- shall engage in matters that please God – Father, Son and Holy Spirit

Case Study

Mobilizing Churches to Respond to HIV/ AIDS: FACT, Zimbabwe

Lorraine Muchaneta

Overview

Organization
FACT (Family AIDS Caring Trust), Zimbabwe

Project description
A community-based response to HIV/AIDS

Issues
HIV/AIDS, mobilizing the local church, sustainability, integral mission

Context

Alice was very frail. For five months a church volunteer cleaned her house, did her laundry and would cook for Alice when she could not do it for herself. One day the volunteer found no one at home. No longer able to pay her rent, Alice had moved to the marketplace. Two days later she was gone. She had died and her body had been taken away by the police.

Mary is 16. Every morning, before going to school, she would clean the house, wash her sick mother and do the cooking. Her father was already dead and she had lost her two brothers. At school Mary was withdrawn and her schoolwork was suffering. Church volunteers started to visit Mary and her mother, helping around the home. As a result, Mary's grades have improved and she is happier at school.

Ruth is also 16. She is an orphan, left to look after her three younger brothers. She is trying to be a good parent to her siblings while continuing to study to be a nurse. One of her brothers is ill most of the time – he is HIV positive. Volunteers visit her and look after her brother so that she can go to school.

Over 40 million people world-wide are infected with HIV. Seventy per cent of the people infected live in sub-Saharan Africa, according to the World Health Organization. Zimbabwe ranks among the top five countries with the highest number of infected people in the southern African region. Twenty-six per cent of its adult population is HIV positive. Between 1,500 and 2,000 people die each week due to HIV-related complications. Zimbabwe's life expectancy, which was 62 in 1990, has dropped to 44 and is expected to drop even further. It is estimated that over 600,000 children have already lost one or both parents to AIDS. Nearly one million will be orphaned as a result of HIV/AIDS within the next four years. There is an urgent need to intensify current efforts to reduce the rate of infection, including mother-to-child transmission.

The prevailing poor social and economic environment in Zimbabwe means the majority of families have to survive against a backdrop of inadequate household food security as well as a decline in the provision of healthcare and other social services.

HIV/AIDS in not just a health problem. It is also a development problem. Merely teaching populations the basics of HIV transmission and the 'ABCs' of prevention (Abstinence, Be faithful and use Condoms) is not enough to change behaviour. Behaviour is influenced deeply by environmental conditions and social norms. Without adequate income, people engage in behaviour that puts them at risk of disease. Without adequate food, diseases progress more rapidly. Without education, social support and the protection of human rights, people become increasingly isolated and vulnerable to disease and discrimination.

Mutare is the third-largest city in Zimbabwe. A third of Mutare's adult population is living with the HIV virus. A community-based mapping exercise to identify orphans and children at risk showed that 25 per cent of households contain children orphaned by AIDS. One in every five households had a sick member of the family or had lost a family member over the last three years.

The church homecare and orphan care programmes target people living with HIV, the terminally ill and children under stress, including orphans. These people come from a variety of religious backgrounds. Because of their social status and the stigma associated with HIV infection they are marginalized and isolated. They lack care and face discrimination. They, especially the women and orphans, are vulnerable to abuse and infection. HIV-related illnesses are long and protracted, and families spend a lot of their few resources seeking treatment for family members.

Description

FACT trains church volunteers and they in turn train family members to care for sick relatives. Volunteers provide home help (bathing, cooking and washing) for clients who have no care-giver or who are being cared for by children. FACT also links clients to health clinics and hospitals. The project runs community-mobilization and awareness-raising campaigns on HIV/AIDS prevention, care and support. FACT is also involved in advocacy, promoting the rights of children and intervening to prevent property grabbing. The project offers pastoral care and bereavement support to clients and their families, including prayer, Bible study, discussion of forgiveness and the assurance of eternal life.

The work with orphans involves supportive home visits from volunteers who have been trained in counselling skills. The counselling provides the orphans with the emotional base to cope with new realities. School fees are provided, together with skills training and income-generating activities. The orphans are given access to temporary relief (food, clothes and shelter). Recreation facilities are provided to assist in mental and physical development. These are provided for both orphans and non-orphans to reduce the stigma attached to being orphaned as a result of AIDS.

Recently, FACT ran its first workshop on parenting skills for children, some as young as 11, who were heading households in which both parents had died. At the end of each day, as the facilitators met to pray and reflect on the day, they sat together and cried.

The overall goal of the project is 'church mobilization for HIV/AIDS prevention, care and support by increasing levels of knowledge about AIDS among church members and promoting caring responses among church members towards people with AIDS, the sick and orphans, empowering communities to care and support the sick and orphans'. The objectives are:

- to sensitize Christian communities on HIV/AIDS issues
- to mobilize church communities to respond to the physical and spiritual needs of people living with HIV/AIDS, the sick and orphans
- to strengthen the ability of individuals, families and communities to cope with HIV infection
- to promote care and compassion for the sick and people living with HIV/AIDS, breaking the silence and resulting in the reduction of stigma, shame and discrimination
- to help families and communities to cope with grief and loss when AIDS has brought death
- to promote HIV/AIDS programming for vulnerable and marginalized children, especially orphans, in order to mitigate the impact

The project started when FACT shared the problem with churches during Sunday services, group fellowships and interdenominational meetings. Workshops were held for church leaders where information on HIV/AIDS and its impact on communities was shared and churches were challenged to respond. One-to-one meetings were also held with individual church leaders to win their support. Once the pastors had caught the vision they invited FACT staff to speak at church services, fellowship group meetings and introduce HIV/AIDS activities in church youth group meetings.

Following this work of raising awareness, invitations were sent to churches to recruit volunteers for training. The response was overwhelming. Within a year 125 volunteers had received training. The FACT homecare programme, which had only 10 per cent of its community referrals from churches, now received 90 per cent of its referral from churches. The homecare project, which used to reach 5 per cent of those who needed homecare support, is now reaching 24 per cent. The number of visits recorded increased from 568 in 1993 to 11,623 in 1998.

Impact

Many churches in the city have been mobilized, particularly the large formal churches. The programme has managed to help churches break down barriers to joint action. AIDS education, care for the sick and support to youths and orphans are now priorities on the church's agenda.

As never before churches are working together on a common programme. It is a rare moment when the church is truly working as the body of Christ, overcoming denominational barriers and reaching out to meet the needs of those in need. In Mutare, volunteers from as many as 46 different church denominations work on a single project.

The mobilization of volunteers from churches has led to improved coverage of homecare services, increased awareness of HIV and the mobilization of other homecare role players. It also means that homecare visits are holistic. There is evidence of reduced unit cost as a result of the involvement of the churches and church volunteers, which strengthens the future sustainability of the programme. The church is addressing the issue of poverty by empowering communities, families and individuals through skills training and helping initiate income-generating projects such as tie-dye cloth production, poultry, pig and goat rearing, market gardening and the provision of seeds and fertilizers.

The programme has led directly to many people receiving Jesus Christ as their personal Saviour and choosing to be baptized and join the church. This includes not only the sick, but often families and caregivers. Most of our AIDS patients make their peace with God by receiving Christ as their personal Saviour before they die. Community attitudes towards the Christian community have changed from indifference to acceptance and respect. Volunteers often wear a T-shirt printed with Isaiah 6:8: '"Whom shall I send? And who will go for us?" And I said, "Here am I. Send me!"' As a result the volunteers are known by a local nickname, meaning 'those who have agreed to be sent' – it has become a term of great respect. This ministry may not add to the growth of the church, since most of these people die shortly after-wards, but each time someone turns to Christ there is joy in heaven and it is sharing this joy that drives us on.

Attitudes towards the involvement of the church by government ministries and community leaders has shifted from that of indifference to active encouragement. There have been numerous calls from the government for the church to take a lead in the promotion of positive behaviour change and in care and support for a nation affected by HIV/AIDS. Within communities in which the project is involved the church has become the uniting force among different sectors of the community because it is the centre of the initiatives.

The Christian community is putting into practice the message of the Great Commission. The church is no longer sitting back and expecting the government to tackle HIV/AIDS-related issues alone. In a hurting world the church is making a positive difference by bringing spiritual healing.

The HIV/AIDS crisis has created an opportunity for the church to reach the poor, the needy, orphans, widows and the unsaved and bring them to a saving knowledge of Christ. As HIV/AIDS sweeps across the nations, leaving in its wake devastated lives, families, communities and nations, the call is for the church to act now.

Evaluation

Initially churches were slow to catch the vision and FACT itself implemented homecare and orphan projects. As a result community ownership of the project was compromised. Sites where FACT has been involved in direct implementation have been difficult to wean. There is a need to invest in building the capacity of communities to enable them to cope.

Successful and sustainable development requires community ownership of the problem and community involvement in the response from planning to implementation. Community ownership of a project starts with sharing the vision through planning, implementation, monitoring and evaluation. In other words, the community must be involved throughout the project cycle. Involving community leadership through committees helps to raise awareness and mobilize resources. Community leaders can initiate and implement interventions and supervise activities. Involving communities in this way means you tap into community knowledge and resources.

Homecare and orphan care should be viewed holistically. Projects need to have a continuum of care, support and prevention that includes the individual, the family and the community as a whole.

External factors affect the project and can impede its achieving its goals. A hostile political climate is leading to a poor economic climate that is in turn fuelling poverty. This affects the most vulnerable groups – the poor, women and children – driving them to engage in risk behaviour, which exposes them to HIV infection and reinfections as they seek means to survive. A decline in healthcare service delivery has led to the unavailability of the free or cheaper healthcare facilities for the poor and a shortage of essential drugs. Many of our homecare patients die at home with no pain relief, often in overcrowded conditions with no proper running water and insufficient food. To overcome the problem of funding FACT is issuing small grants to enable communities to start self-help projects.

The church has now taken HIV/AIDS issues as a priority. This was achieved through HIV/AIDS education, awareness, mobilization and involvement. HIV/AIDS has not remained outside the church as Christians had believed it would in the past. The churches that are still reluctant to participate include those in which faith healing is the principle intervention in times of sickness.

The role of FACT is to facilitate the process of community mobilization through the church. FACT builds community awareness and assists communities to develop care strategies. It is important to strengthen the capacity of households and communities to find solutions to the problems affecting people living with HIV/AIDS.

Summary of lessons learned

- strategies need to be relevant to both community needs and existing sociocultural practices
- sustainable, low-cost programmes require community empowerment and capacity building
- it is important to respect confidentiality and use of non-discriminatory approaches
- volunteers should not be exploited and burnout should be prevented
- the goal should be sustainability in terms of funding, human resources and total ownership by the community

Colin was an eight-year-old orphan with HIV. He was unable to stay with his relatives because they did not want him – they were worried he would infect their own children – so he was admitted to hospital. The doctor who referred him to me said, 'Lorraine, he needs love.' So I visited him, expecting to give him love, but he gave me abundant love. I thought I was going to witness to him, but he witnessed to me. As he prayed – not for himself, but for me – he taught me about courage and love, and about how God can use even a frail, sick child.

Part Four

Integral Mission, Advocacy and Lifestyle

Integral Mission and Advocacy

Gary A Haugen

As the church of Jesus Christ enters its third millennium, many who have led the church in preaching the gospel to the ends of the earth and in providing for the needy are sensing the leading of the Holy Spirit into another frontier of ministry. The church is perceiving that hurting people not only need the word and bread, they need a voice as well. This work of providing a voice for the voiceless is referred to by many as the ministry of advocacy. Advocacy is a response to the biblical exhortation of Proverbs 31:8–9:

> Speak up for those who cannot speak for themselves,
> for the rights of all who are destitute.
> Speak up and judge fairly;
> defend the rights of the poor and needy.

Indeed, the Spirit is inviting the church into a new era of advocacy that is as significant as the global missions movement of the past 150 years and the relief and development movement of the past 50 years. The need is no less great, nor the biblical mandate any less fundamental.

At this historic moment our greatest need is for clarity of vision about this call to advocacy. The church's response to the call to advocacy is threatened by two opposite hindrances to obedience – paralysing ignorance and paralysing sophistication. On the one hand, many in the body of Christ are ignorant of the call. We do not see the need or know what is required of us. So God tells us simply: Love me. Love your neighbour. Do justice. Love mercy. Walk humbly. On the other hand, we are tempted into the paralysis of sophistication, threatened by an approach to advocacy that becomes intellectually rarefied, operationally remote and overly sophisticated in a way that alienates, confuses and immobilizes much of the body of Christ. We need to ask God to help us make it clear to the Christian community that the work of advocacy is desperately needed, thoroughly biblical and eminently doable.

Finding Clarity through our Neighbour's Story

The biblical call to advocacy emerges with straight-forward simplicity from Christ's command to love our neighbour. Jesus said that all of the law and the prophets were summed up in the command to love God and to love our neighbour as ourselves (Mt. 22:35–40). The lawyer of Luke 10 was able to repeat to Jesus this correct answer. But finding, as we all do, that the right answer is easier to recite than to obey, the lawyer ran for cover by suggesting that the whole matter was more complicated than Jesus allowed. Undeterred, Jesus pressed the point home with unrelenting clarity by telling a simple story about a man lying, beaten, on the road to Jericho (Lk. 10:30–37). What, Jesus asked, would a person who loved the wounded man do in such a situation?

Through the simplicity of story Jesus sweeps away sophisticated diversions. He confronts us with the clear facts about an individual human being in need and asks: What does love require? Likewise, the biblical call to advocacy emerges with singular clarity through simple stories about neighbours in need – stories that force us to ask: What does love require?

I would like to offer the stories of five neighbours from around the world and ask of the body of Christ: What does love require?

Joyti is a 14-year-old girl from a rural town in India who was abducted and drugged by four women who sold her into a brothel in Bombay. She was locked away in an underground cell and severely beaten with metal rods, plastic pipe and electrical cords until submitting to provide sex to the customers. Now she must work 7 days a week, servicing 20–40 customers a day.

Osner is a 45-year-old man in Haiti who was illegally arrested and thrown in prison when the local mayor wanted to seize part of his land for her personal use. The detention is completely illegal under Haitian law and five different court orders have been issued demanding Osner's release, but the prison authorities refuse to release him because of their political relationship with the mayor.

Shama is a ten-year-old girl who was sold into bonded slavery for a family debt of $35, which was incurred to pay for her mother's medical treatment. As a result, for the last three years, Shama has been forced to work six days a week, 12–14 hours a day, rolling cigarettes by hand. She must roll 2,000 cigarettes a day or else she gets beaten. Her bonded slavery is completely illegal under Indian law, but local authorities do not enforce the law.

Domingo is an elderly peasant farmer in Honduras who was shot in the face and leg when police illegally opened fire on him and other Lenca Indians while they were marching in the capital city for better government services in their remote region. The President of Honduras issued a promise to compensate all the injured, but nearly a year has gone by and the payments have never come. Now Domingo has lost his house and land because he is disabled and cannot work to make the payments.

Catherine is a 13-year-old girl who lives in a Manila slum and cannot go to school because her aunt forces her to work as a domestic servant. Worse, Catherine's aunt allows some of her male friends to live in the house and one of them raped Catherine while everyone else was out of the home. Catherine managed to file a complaint with the police, but the rapist is the son of a policeman and they have ignored the order to arrest the man for two years.

Identifying Our Neighbour's Needs

If followers of Jesus Christ are to respond in love to each of his people, the first task is to identify the nature of their needs. In the early days of the modern missionary movement evangelicals focused on responding to those who needed to *hear* the gospel. Heroic strides have been made in the verbal proclamation of the gospel over the last century-and-a-half. And it remains true today that we certainly do not love our neighbours well if we do not explain to them the gospel truth.

Yet the evangelical missionary movement grievously erred to the extent that it failed to respond in love to the other needs of its neighbours. As early as 1947 the evangelical theologian Carl FH Henry challenged an evangelism of mere words, insisting that: 'There is no room for a gospel that is indifferent to the needs of the total man or the global man.'[64]

The effort expended by the missional church in meeting physical and social needs was miniscule in proportion to the clarity of the biblical mandate to meet such needs. It was wrong, and it set back the advancement of the gospel. This began to change in the later part of the twentieth century. A new generation of evangelical leaders returned the church to a biblical view of evangelism that ministered to the whole person. Evangelicalism embraced a witness in which the verbal proclamation of the gospel and care for our neighbour's physical and social needs are, in the words of the *Lausanne Covenant* of 1974, 'both part of our Christian duty'. Over the last generation, the evangelical community has developed tremendous capacities to respond to those who suffer from deprivation – those who are hurting because of their lack of food, clean water, medical care, shelter, schools, etc. In the year 2000 evangelical relief and development organizations in the United States alone spent more than \$1 billion in responding to deprivation in our world.[65]

But this is where the old era ends and the new era of justice advocacy begins. In our five simple stories we see a different category of people who are hurting in our world. The traditional ministries of the evangelical community do not respond to their needs. They are not suffering today because they have not heard the gospel or do not have a church among their people. And so we do not

---

[64] Carl FH Henry, *The Uneasy Conscience of Modern Fundamentalism* (Grand Rapids, Michigan: Eerdmans, 1947)

[65] World Vision, World Relief, World Concern, Compassion International, The Salvation Army, Food for the Hungry, Action International, Samaritan's Purse, Food for the Poor and Habitat for Humanity.

show meaningful love to them in their situation by merely bringing the gifts of verbal evangelism. Nor are they suffering because of deprivation. None of them are hurting because they do not have food, shelter or healthcare. They are in a different category of need. They are suffering because they have an oppressor. They are hurting because they have bullies who abuse them. They are victims of injustice. And, for the most part, the existing ministries of the evangelical community do not provide meaningful help at their point of need.

This, then, is the vast new frontier of justice advocacy. And it would be difficult to identify another area of ministry where there is such a disparity between the magnitude of the need, the clarity of the biblical mandate and the dearth of actual ministry.

The Magnitude of the Need

Let us first clarify the nature and magnitude of the need. To do so it is important to reinforce the distinction between those who suffer from *deprivation* and those who suffer from *oppression*. We meet the needs of those who suffer deprivation – the lack of access to some material good – by providing material goods or services. But those who suffer oppression are hurting because they are victimized by the sin of injustice. The Bible defines this as the abuse of power. It is taking from others what God has given them – their life, liberty, the fruit of their love and the fruit of their labour. We cannot respond to this need simply by providing them with some material good. To show authentic love to the victim of oppression we must rescue them from their oppressor, bring the perpetrator to account, seek the restoration of the victim and prevent the abuse happening again.

If you love Joyti, you must try to get her out of the brothel. If you love Osner, you must seek his release from prison. If you love Shama, you must release her from slavery. If you love Domingo or Catherine, you must seek justice for them. This is what love requires. Yet this is not what most evangelical mission or development agencies do. While it may not be appropriate for every organization to take up this role, our clear biblical mandate suggests that somebody in the body of Christ certainly should.

This, then, is a distinctive need – different from those who suffer from not hearing the gospel and different from those who suffer deprivation. But what is the magnitude of the need? How many people in our world suffer because of the oppressive power of others?

There are at least a million children taken into forced prostitution every year. In countries like Haiti and Honduras 85 per cent of those held in prisons and jails have never been charged or convicted of a crime. In India alone there are at least ten million children who are held illegally in bonded slavery. Thousands of impoverished women and children in the developing world are sexually assaulted every year without anyone investigating the crime.

Add to these statistics events like the Rwandan genocide in 1994 in which 800,000 people were murdered in eight weeks. How, if at all, did the Christians of the world manifest the love of Christ to these neighbours? As director of the United Nations' genocide investigation in Rwanda, I sorted through the corpses of thousands of Tutsi women and children. As they huddled in terror for protection in the churches of Rwanda they did not need Bibles, sermons, food, medicine or housing materials. They needed a voice. They needed a voice that would move the world to restrain their machete-wielding

Hutu neighbours. They needed an international security operation whose feasibility is unquestioned by subsequent military analysis.

The masses of people suffering because of oppression and abuse is as large, if not larger, than any other category of need in the world. In 1996 the International Justice Mission conducted a study among 70 evangelical mission and development organizations representing thousands of workers around the world. We asked them if they had workers serving in communities where people suffer injustice and abuse under circumstances in which local authorities could not be relied upon for relief. *All* of the agencies said they did. The most common categories of injustice included:

- public justice corruption
- abusive police or military
- child prostitution
- detention or disappearance without charge or trial
- state-supported discrimination or abuse of ethnic minorities
- organized political intimidation
- state-sponsored torture
- abusive child labour
- corrupt seizure or extortion of land
- forced migration
- forced adult or teenage prostitution
- extortion or withholding of wages
- organized racial violence
- state-sponsored religious persecution
- murder of street children
- child pornography
- state, rebel or paramilitary terrorism
- genocide

In the course of Christian ministry around the world we have learned a lot about the needs of our global neighbours – especially the needs of the poor. They go hungry, they get sick, they go without shelter. But we have also learned that they get abused by others.

The World Bank recently released an extensive study of the experiences of the poor. The multi-volume work is entitled *Voices of the Poor* and was constructed out of personal interviews with tens of thousands of poor people around the globe. The authors repeatedly emphasize the major role oppression and abuse play in the experience of the poor:

> Perhaps one of the most striking revelations of the study is the extent to which the police and official justice systems side with the rich, persecute poor people and make poor people more insecure, fearful, and poorer … Women report feeling vulnerable to sexual assault by police, and young men say that they have been beaten up by the police without cause.[66]

The Clarity of the Biblical Mandate

There can be little doubt about the staggering number of people suffering injustice and who are desperately in need of advocacy. Likewise, there can be no doubt about the clarity of the biblical mandate to respond to this need. It should be sufficient simply to cite Jesus' command to love our neighbour and allow the logic of the 'golden rule' to direct us in our response to someone being raped, tortured, imprisoned, pushed off their land or beaten up.

---

[66] Deepa Narayan, Meera Shah, Patt Petesch and Robert Chambers, *Voices of the Poor: Crying Out for Change* volume 2, (Oxford: Oxford University Press/World Bank, 2000), 163

If this were happening to us we would want someone to rescue us. This is the logic of the author of Hebrews:

> Remember those who are in prison, as though you were in prison with them; those who are being tortured, as though you yourselves were being tortured. (Heb. 13:3, NRSV)

If Jesus' greatest commandment were not enough, we have the word of the Lord calling us to 'seek justice, rescue the oppressed, defend the orphan, plead for the widow' (Is. 1:17, NRSV). The Old Testament prophets make clear that when we do not pursue justice God despises our sacrifices and prayers (Is. 1), our fasting (Is. 58) and our religious festivals (Amos 5). Jesus himself rebuked the religious leaders of his day for neglecting the 'weightier matters of the law: justice, mercy and faith' (Mt. 23:23).

We could tour through the Scriptures documenting God's passion for justice and his call to his people to 'rescue the weak and the needy; deliver them from the hand of the wicked' (Ps. 82:4). Given the extensive nature of the need and the clarity of the biblical mandate, one would expect an extensive deployment of God's people to meet the needs of the abused and the oppressed. Would that it were so.

The Dearth of Actual Ministry

The reality is that the level of engagement in seeking justice, rescuing the oppressed, defending the orphan and pleading for the widow is small compared to the need and the biblical mandate. If one simply looks at the categories of abuse identified above in the International Justice Mission survey, one would be hard-pressed to identify any category that is the primary operational focus of an existing evangelical mission or development organization. The International Justice Mission drew out of the study's findings that none of the agencies felt equipped to deal with these issues, nor were they aware of any faith-based agency to which they could turn for help. There were indications that the agencies felt they could get some assistance in issues of religious persecution, but this created some unease about the perception that the only time Christians engaged in justice issues was when they themselves were the victims. Consider again the needs of Joyti, Osner, Shama, Domingo and Catherine. What percentage of the churches' resources are being deployed to the rescue of the victims of forced prostitution, illegal detention, torture, police abuse, child slavery or other abusive conditions?

Over recent years a number of Christian ministries – especially in the development field – have begun to appreciate the problems of oppression and have begun to engage advocacy programmes to speak for issues such as Third World debt, conflict diamonds, sex trafficking, child soldiers and child labour. These efforts are promising developments that represent a maturing of the evangelical vision.

Yet agencies involved in this new engagement in advocacy have tended to do so at the fairly rarefied level of public policy advocacy. They have taken on macro-level issues and sought to mobilize public policy élites to pursue structural policy solutions. There is much that is right about this and, indeed, more should be done. The body of Christ has started in the field of advocacy by doing what it knows how to do – public policy research, awareness campaigns and lobbying.

Nevertheless, there are important differences between ministry to individual victims of oppression and issue-based advocacy. If we consider the plights of Joyti, Osner, Shama, Domingo and Catherine and ask how we might most effectively rescue them from their suffering, we would not opt for issue-based advocacy (public policy research, awareness campaigns and lobbying). We would instead be lead to what we might call 'case advocacy' – the diverse set of tasks that can be pursued to bring rescue and justice for a victim of abuse and oppression.

By way of example, let us consider the methods by which the International Justice Mission pursued case advocacy in each of our stories.

- Criminal investigators were used to infiltrate the brothel where Joyti was being held. Video surveillance technology was used to document where she was being held, and by whom. Secure police contacts were mobilized to raid the brothel and release Joyti. Joyti was referred to a place of residential Christian aftercare; her brothel keeper was arrested and is facing prosecution.
- American and Haitian lawyers were used in Osner's case to develop legal proofs that his detention was illegal. These were presented to the United States State Department and Congress to secure his release from the uncooperative Haitian authorities.
- Shama's bonded slavery was professionally investigated and documented, exposing a syndicate of over 400 other bonded slaves. Lawyers intervened with the local magistrate through indigenous relationships, obtaining the release of all the child slaves and the arrest of the moneylenders. Shama and the other children were subsequently given the opportunity to go to school.
- In Domingo's case a Honduran attorney was hired to prepare an advocacy package for the President with the support of American lawyers. Within one week of

receiving the documents, Domingo and all the 40 victims received full compensation payments.

- A Christian lawyer provided free services for Catherine as a private prosecutor, obtained the arrest of the assailant and secured his prosecution.

Each one of these cases involves a victim who is part of larger structural injustice that needs to be addressed through issue-based advocacy. But in our appreciation of the structural and political nature of these problems, we should not leapfrog over the victims and the opportunities to rescue millions of needy neighbours. Nor should we neglect the opportunities that exist to resource indigenous Christians for the work of case advocacy within their own communities. Not only does case advocacy provide the best source of the street-level intelligence necessary for effective public policy work, it provides a concrete witness of tangible love to actual individuals.

We should not underestimate what can be achieved out of a limited imagination for the diverse gifts God has placed in the body of Christ. Many Christians who are active in mission, development or issue-based advocacy would see little hope for the five victims featured in these stories. But for Christian public justice professionals, these cases represent precisely the kinds of problems they know how to solve. We should pray that the Lord mobilizes the vast human and financial resources of legal and law enforcement professionals to serve the victims of oppression.

Conclusion

May God grant us the capacity to provide a clear vision for the ministry of justice advocacy and the courage to walk in that sacrificial calling. May we make plain the urgent needs of the voiceless in our world, the biblical invitation to the joy of service and the great hope that God does not give us a ministry for which he will not empower us. In so doing we will point people to the love of Jesus. As David Bosch wrote:

> [Jesus] did not soar off into heavenly heights but immersed himself into the altogether real circumstances of the poor, the captives, the blind, the oppressed. Today, too, Christ is where the hungry and the sick are, the exploited and the marginalized. The power of his resurrection propels human history toward the end, under the banner 'Behold, I make all things new!' Like its Lord, the church-in-mission must take sides, *for* life and against death, *for* justice and against oppression.[67]

---

[67] Bosch, *Transforming Mission*, 426.

Integral Mission, Humility and Lifestyle

A Summary by Tim Chester based on a Presentation by CB Samuel

The subject of humility might appear out of place in a discussion of integral mission and Christian development. But according to Micah 6:8 walking humbly before the Lord is as much a requirement of God as seeking justice and showing kindness. God repeatedly warns his people against the sin of pride. Humility is close to God's heart. God esteems those who are humble and brings down the proud.

Humility is important because pride is so natural for us. If you want to grow weeds you do not need to do anything, but if you want to grow rice you must cultivate it. It is the same with pride and humility. Pride grows naturally, but humility must be cultivated. But this does not mean adopting certain outward postures. Humility cannot be reduced to external actions – it is the inner environment of the heart. It is a characteristic of a person who is secure in God. And walking humbly is about corporate life as well as a personal walk. As development agencies we can too easily want to promote our successes and find it hard to celebrate the achievements of others.

I want to highlight a number of ways in which humility is crucial to the task of integral mission.

1. Humility and the Marginalized

There are many ways in which we can look at the poor. We can see them as statistics, as objects of charity or as victims of injustice. But true humility is seeing the poor as those who represent God. We can too easily have professional concern for the poor from nine-to-five, but then want nothing to do with them. Mother Teresa said that every foot she tended she looked on as the foot of Jesus.

The story is told of a man who died and went to heaven. To his surprise he found there was a bank in heaven. But when he went to make a withdrawal he was told he had no funds in his account. How, he asked, could he have made deposits when there were no branches on earth? 'Did you not read Jesus' words?' the clerk replied. 'Give to the poor and you will receive treasure in heaven. The poor are the representatives of the bank of heaven.' As he was pondering these words, a development worker came in to make his first withdrawal, but he too found he had no funds. 'You deposited a lot of money with the poor', explained the bank clerk, 'but none of it was yours.'

God gives us an opportunity to know him more through the poor. We lose out when we do not read the word of God with the poor of the world. We must see the poor not as objects of charity, but as people from whom we can learn.

2. Humility and Transformation

Jesus said: 'Blessed are the meek, for they will inherit the earth' (Mt. 5:5). He came into Jerusalem on a donkey to send the message that the world belongs to those who are humble. We need to ask whether we and our organizations reflect a culture of humility, for humility is the approach of the kingdom. There are many ways of exercising power in our world – through money, power and prestige. But Jesus taught us that meekness is the way to exercise power in the kingdom of God. Humility is God's method for changing the world. The one who reigns on the throne of heaven is the Lamb who was slain.

In 2 Corinthians 4:7 Paul says we have God's treasure in earthen vessels. Transformation is only possible through broken vessels. We need to find room for broken people in our organizations and communities. Then the ordinary people of the world will say of us that we are their kind of community. Communities of hope are communities of broken people.

3. Humility and Leadership

When he washed his disciples' feet, Jesus gave us a model of leadership. Humility is a style of leadership in which we build the people whom we serve. This is borne out of a secure relationship with God. In India there is a saying: 'If you are meek, people will sit on your head' – they will exploit your humility. But humility is the only model we have been given by God. In 1 Corinthians 4 Paul says that the apostles are 'at the end of the procession'. They are 'the scum of the earth'. This is authentic Christian leadership. If you choose to be irrelevant you are not out of touch. You are where most of the world is. The poor of the world are not relevant. When we become the scum of the world we become what the poor already are.

Moses was called the most humble of men. It was said of him at a time when Miriam and Aaron were opposing him. Humility is perhaps tested most when people criticize you. Moses' response was not to retaliate, but to intercede for them. Humble leadership is also reflected in a willingness to co-operate with others. Too often our instinct is to compete with others, but people of humility work with one another.

4. Humility and Lifestyle

The problem with lifestyle is not its theory, but its practice. The story is told of an Indian guru who taught his disciples to live on just the basic necessities of life. One day he sent his best disciple out to make his own way in the world. This disciple owned only two loincloths – one to wear while the other was washed. And so this disciple lived, each day wearing one cloth while he washed the other. One day a rat ate his spare cloth as it hung out to dry. His neighbours gave him another, but he realized he also needed a cat to keep the rat away. And because the cat needed milk he got a cow. To feed the cow he obtained a small piece of land for fodder. Soon he was hiring people to cultivate the land so he did not have to interrupt his meditations. In time he acquired a large estate and a fine house. One day his guru came by. Seeing the large house, he asked his disciple how this had happened. The disciple said: 'I need all this to protect my loincloth.'

When many of us were young Christians we committed ourselves to radical lifestyles. But now we have many justifications for the possessions that over time we have acquired. We need to recover a biblical perspective on wealth and money. Jesus sees money as a spiritual force. He says we need consciously to short-circuit its power in our lives. Jacques Ellul said that Jesus was the only one who was prepared to describe money as mammon.

We need to define limits for consumption. We evangelicals have a theology for the creation and distribution of wealth, but we need to have a theology of consumption. We need to define what is enough. We need to learn that we do not need to own everything. We need to explore the possibilities of sharing with others and owning things communally.

Humility is not an option for those committed to holistic ministry. Humility is the strength of transformation. Humility is central to the character of Jesus. Humility is a characteristic God wants all of us to have. Jesus said: 'Learn from me, for I am gentle and humble in heart' (Mt. 11:29).

Case Study

The Rights of Indigenous Peoples and Environmental Protection: MOPAWI, Honduras

Oswaldo E Munguía

Overview

Organization
MOPAWI (Mosquitia Pawisa, 'Development of the Mosquitia'), Honduras

Project description
A campaign to prevent the construction of a dam that threatened environmental destruction and the land rights of indigenous people

Issues
Advocacy, lobbying, multinational corporations, indigenous peoples, land rights, the environment

Context

The Mosquitia is a vast region, making up a quarter of the area of Honduras, with various natural ecosystems. It is inhabited by five ethnic peoples: Miskitos, Tawahka, Pech, Garifuna and Mestizo, better known locally as Ladino. The population of 110,000 (less than 2 per cent of the national population) found itself confronted with the process of transition from a subsistence economy to a market economy. The population of the Mosquitia is officially recognized as one of the poorest of the country, in spite of inhabiting a region with rich natural resources. Its poverty is linked to the high level of illiteracy (over 50 per cent) and poor educational services. While most of the indigenous peoples of Honduras have lost their language, the geographical isolation of the Mosquitia has preserved much Honduran culture and language.

Recent moves to a market economy are threatening the natural resources of the region. Foreign capital, for example, is hiring local people to fish local species of lobster and snail, potentially driving these species to extinction. Local people believe their poverty is due to the lack of employment, making them vulnerable to any offer of jobs. They will accept exploitation of their natural resources if this brings in some income. This will continue until their land rights are recognized and a political and legal system is set up to respect this property.

MOPAWI was established on Christian principles in 1985 to reduce poverty in the Mosquitia area through sustainable agriculture, preventive community health-care and micro-enterprise. MOPAWI soon discovered that the destruction of the region's natural resources posed a greater threat to its population. MOPAWI realized that the social structure was poorly organized or non-existent. It therefore started a programme to foster and create community organizations. Working with MOPAWI, the five ethnic groups of the region have in recent years introduced bilingual primary education, formed indigenous political organizations, lobbied to reduce deforestation and are in the process of achieving some important successes on land right claims. Fifteen years ago integral mission could not have been imagined. But the process of claiming land rights has developed local skills, community participation and the capacity of the community to respond to outside threats, as the case of the Patuca II Dam demonstrates.

Description

In the 1970s Honduras built its largest ever hydroelectrical project, *El Cajón*. The dam not only supplied sufficient energy for national needs, it produced a surplus for other countries in the region. But in 1994 the longest-ever dry season, the result of forest degradation, meant it could no longer meet demand and electricity was rationed. Meanwhile neighbouring countries put pressure on the Honduran government to present schemes for the regional interconnection.

The government had regarded the Patuca and Rio Sico rivers in the Mosquitia as possible hydroelectric resources since the 1960s. In 1995 they contracted two American companies to build the Patuca II Dam with a 40-year concession to sell electricity to the state electricity company. The proposed site for construction was Patuca Medio. It lay between two areas which for seven years we had been waiting to be declared protected areas. The process had remained entangled in bureaucratic paper-work. Construction companies were hired without any reliable study of the environmental impact. Downriver

10,000 indigenous Miskitos and Tawahka would be affected. A 60-kilometre road was to be built, plus a camp-site for the 3,000 workers. The dam threatened to cause incalculable damage to the indigenous populations of the Mosquitia and to alter radically the ecosystems of the tropical rainforests – the remaining 'continuous' natural areas in which the indigenous populations still live.

MOPAWI recognized the need to warn the people of the region at all levels about the implications of the construction. Drawing on its links with a wide range of environmental, development and human rights organizations, MOPAWI formed a coalition that also included local governments and indigenous organizations. A detailed study of the project was conducted, with expert advice in hydrology, geology and large-scale construction. The years spent developing the organizational skills of the population were now going to be put to good use.

MOPAWI organized seminars, conferences and work-shops to raise awareness of the issue. A weekly local radio programme allowed people to express their reservations about the project. MOPAWI lobbied the central govern-ment and the building companies to abandon the project. It drew attention to the evidence showing the non-viability of the project, the risks involved and the irreversible chaos it would cause. We used private discussions, press confer-ences and a public forum in the capital that brought together the government, the building companies, leaders of the indigenous organizations, environmental groups and the media. We also contacted the World Bank and the Inter-American Development Bank, together with other international investment organizations, in order to inform them fully about the financial hazards involved in building a dam in that area and the social and environmental conse-quences. MOPAWI also involved associated organizations in the United Kingdom and the United States to exert external pressure on the Honduran government and the construction companies.

Results

As a result of the campaign the dam became an issue of national interest. When the companies realized that our arguments were well founded they became interested in dialogue. The coalition did not just protest against the construction of the dam. We also offered alternative solutions. We recognized the need to generate electricity and showed that a series of small dams built all over the country, together with the use of solar, aeolian energy and energy from compost, could provide sufficient electricity for the whole population. In October 1998 Hurricane Mitch swept over Honduras, causing enormous damage to housing and the environment. A survey conducted after the hurricane showed that even if the dam had survived the impact of the hurricane and resultant flooding, the debris would have made it unusable.

In March 1999 the companies withdrew from the Patuca II project. They said their decision was due to the intense local opposition. We believe it was also because they saw its non-viability. At the end of 1999 the National Congress granted Patuca Medio the status of protected area. The World Bank, through its Global Environment Facilities, has initiated a programme for the preservation of the biodiversity in the reserve. In January 2001 MOPAWI set up a pilot study looking at the restoration of a micro-basin in association with a project of sustainable development with the local population.

Impact

Today it seems clear that a large dam should not be built in the Patuca National Park and that initiatives should be put in place for the preservation of the environment and sustainable development. But it has taken years of sustained effort to reach the point where indigenous people have the confidence to claim property rights and to participate in the decision making. The indigenous populations are regaining self-esteem and pride of their culture. They are in the process of reaching a state of equality as creatures made in the image of God. From being ignored 20 years ago, community organizations are now strong enough to claim their rights and negotiate at the highest levels of government. They are making alliances with specialist agencies.

The campaigns have helped to bring together indigenous and non-indigenous communities who share the same conditions of poverty. They have understood that they share the same agenda and that they can achieve more by working together. The relationship with the world of business still requires attention. Not all the enterprises in the region realize the importance of recognizing indigenous people as citizens with equal rights.

Evaluation

The campaign taught us the importance of:

• working in coalition with all the groups affected – community organizations, local governments, specialist development and environmental agencies

- having a good knowledge of the issue – the nature of the problem, your allies and opponents, and the strengths and weaknesses of your case
- maintaining a continuous and transparent dialogue between leaders, communities and allies
- studying carefully the case for and against the issue with the help of professional specialists

In this way we built a case that caught the attention of major players. Opposition to the dam grew and consolidated. Finally, the damage wrought by Hurricane Mitch showed the campaign was correct to question the viability of the dam. The construction companies perhaps recognized that the campaign gave them the opportunity to avoid financial disaster.

Case Study

Defending Innocent Prisoners:
Peace and Hope, Peru

Alfonso Wieland

Overview

Organization
Peace and Hope (Paz y Esperanza), Peru

Project description
Providing legal support to innocent prisoners

Issues
Advocacy, human rights, campaigning, media

Context

Since the 1980s Peru has suffered a bloody civil conflict. Although terrorist violence has significantly diminished, the much-longed-for peace has not been realized, nor has national reconciliation taken place. Over 30,000 people died as victims of the violence, many were tortured, 5,000 disappeared, about 600,000 were displaced, thousands are detained and over 18,000 innocent men and women, many of them evangelicals, were unjustly thrown into prisons.

According to reports from Peru's National Penitentiary Institute and from the Defender of the People, of the 21,785 Peruvians detained since 1992 for presumed terrorist crimes and treason, 18,000 are innocent. Many of them, often Quechuan-speaking land workers, have been absolved at trial. But a great many were sentenced to 10, 20 or 30 years' imprisonment and some even to life sentences.

The tragedy of Peru's innocent detainees significantly worsened in 1992. In the wake of political violence and a *coup d'état*, then-president Alberto Fujimori created Law 25475 on terrorism and Law 25659 on treason under the pretext of combating terrorism. These laws, which violate human rights, are still in force today. Coupled with a corrupt justice administration, they led to the imprisonment of innocent people. Through these laws many 'presumed repentant terrorists' gained their liberty by giving the names of 'presumed subversive individuals'.

On 17 August 1996, under pressure from human rights organizations, evangelical churches and Catholic churches, President Fujimori created an Ad-Hoc Commission to investigate the cases of people unfairly condemned for terrorism and treason. This commission was presided over by the Defender of the People. Hundreds of prisoners were set free at trial and others won their freedom through presidential reprieve.

Description

Starting in 1996, Peace and Hope took up the legal defence of innocent prisoners together with national and international campaigns to make people aware of the problem. The aims were:

- to obtain government reprieves for innocent detainees
- to secure the freedom of innocent detainees whose cases came before the Ad-Hoc Commission
- the cancellation of the criminal records of innocent detainees
- the re-establishment of the civil rights of innocent detainees
- for the whole society to seek pardon for what had been done

Working with human rights organizations, churches, lawyers, the media and international NGOs, Peace and Hope sought to overcome the resistance of Fujimori's political regime, and police and judicial power. It was important to mobilize support at the right time – when cases came before the Ad-Hoc Commission or when names for reprieve were presented to the president. The campaign faced a lack of sensitivity to the issue from the population and experienced the dangers of fighting for the innocent.

Peace and Hope was the only evangelical body that dedicated its efforts to defend men and women unjustly accused of terrorism. Many of the cases we took up were those of evangelicals, although this was not an essential requirement. The only essential requirement was a person's innocence. The church had a very important role. It organized prayer campaigns, religious services and public demonstrations.

Results

Between 1996 and 1999 the Ad-Hoc Commission put before President Fujimori 513 cases of innocent people condemned for terrorism and treason. All 513 represented juridical errors by the previous government. In December 1999 the Ad-Hoc Commission transferred responsibility for the review of innocent prisoners to the National Council for Human Rights, a branch of the Justice Ministry. But, due to lack of political will, this process was delayed for almost one year. After the fall of Fujimori's government, the transitional government of Valentín Paniagua reactivated the reprieve process through the National Council for Human Rights, and as of January 2001 a further 200 innocent prisoners have been released.

The attitude of the population towards innocent prisoners has changed. The people in Peru have no doubt now that those who were reprieved are innocent. The criminal records of prisoners who have been found innocent have been cancelled on their release. The issue of innocent prisoners has been incorporated into the Truth Commission (Comisión de la Verdad), which will investigate the last 20 years of political violence. The commission has a mandate to punish those responsible and seek compensation for the victims. Over 80 evangelicals have been reprieved and hundreds were absolved at trial.

Impact

Many unjustly imprisoned Christians have been released. Peace and Hope is recognized around the world as the only human rights evangelical organization that defended innocent prisoners in Peru and carried out its ministry in the prisons of highest security. Peace and Hope is a permanent member of the National Council for Human Rights and its initiatives are taken into account.

The defence of the innocent prisoners played an educational role in many churches. They realized that the search of justice and the defence of the innocent is a biblical imperative. A national and international solidarity network was created, which, if need be, can work on other issues.

Evaluation

Looking back, we could have lobbied opinion leaders directly – we lacked strong political support. We did not work closely enough with the church – we would have benefited from greater involvement from the church. Although we did provide some pastoral care for prisoners and their families, we did not develop a strategy for spiritual support. We were also unable to put in place social and post-release support for the reprieved.

Our work was hampered by the lack of interest of the government and a corrupt justice system than obstructed the investigation of each case. A lack of information allowed members of the government to manipulate public opinion against the innocent.

An important factor in our work was our clear understanding of working side by side with secular human rights organizations and the Catholic church. We developed ways to interact with these organizations while expressing our faith and sharing Christian values.

The national and international pressure on the government was another key factor in changing attitudes towards innocent prisoners. We worked closely with the media, making sure they were correctly informed. The involvement of relatives and the innocents themselves was important for the success of the campaign. They contributed ideas and participated actively in demonstrations, prayer meetings, media reports and so on. It was the dramatic testimony of the individuals involved that touched the hearts of public opinion. It was important to raise the issue at a political level because we could not obtain justice through the judiciary alone.

Case Study

Campaigning for Macro-Policy Change: Jubilee 2000

Ann Pettifor

Overview

Organization
Jubilee 2000 Coalition

Project description
International campaign for debt relief

Issues
Advocacy, campaigning, networking, mobilizing grass-roots action

Context

In 1996 – the year in which the Jubilee 2000 campaign began – Third World debt was not only crippling the development of poorer countries, it was shifting that development into reverse. The people of Africa owed more in international debt than their annual income. The debts were the result of irresponsible lending, corrupt regimes kept in place by cold war politics, rises in the price of oil and a global economic and trading system that favoured powerful countries. It was the poor who were paying the price, even though they had had little say in the decision to take out the debts and had seen little benefit from them. The cost of servicing the debt led to cuts in health and education. Western development aid was flowing back to the West in debt repayments. And the remedies imposed by the IMF and World Bank seemed to be making things worse rather than better – at least for the poor.

Description

The spark that led to the Jubilee 2000 campaign was the idea of making the year 2000 a year of debt relief. Drawing on the biblical idea of jubilee (Lev. 25, Deut. 15), the campaign called for a debt-free start to the millennium for a billion people through the cancellation of the unpayable debts of the world's poorest countries.

In the UK the Jubilee 2000 Coalition brought together over 100 different groups including aid agencies, churches, trade unions and women's groups. A further 68 coalitions were formed around the world, in both the north and the south.

Results

The world will never be the same again. In just four years of sustained campaigning and solidarity building, the international Jubilee 2000 movement persuaded the world's most powerful leaders to write off over $100 billion of debt and free up new resources for poverty reduction in debtor nations. We transformed the global debate about debt, international finance and development. But we did more than that. We transformed the way in which millions of people approach international finance, and gave these people the competence and confidence to challenge élites in both the north and the south.

A recalcitrant US Congress was obliged to contribute substantial sums towards a trust fund to finance debt relief, and to remove conditions for users. The movement forced G7 governments to introduce poverty reduction concepts into the economic programmes of the IMF. While much of the debate about poverty reduction remains tokenistic, the movement in support of debtor nations has intensified critiques of neo-liberal ideology and IMF economic programmes.

Jubilee 2000 helped build broad-based coalitions in countries where unity around development issues was previously unknown. The Jubilee 2000 petition, which entered the *Guinness Book of Records* as the first petition to be signed in more than 150 countries, was backed by close to 20 million people.

Impact

Perhaps the movement's greatest achievement has been the building of international solidarity between citizens in the north and south. This in turn has given confidence to southern leaders. Through the G77, OPEC (Organization of Petroleum Exporting Countries) and other fora, southern leaders have begun to stand up for the rights of their indebted nations and to demand justice in sovereign debtor and creditor relationships.

Another achievement has been to make the international financial system more transparent. The Paris club – the club of creditors – is secretive, but we made it famous. In the Paris club the creditors are the plaintiff, the judge, the jury and the executioner. They had a rule that any debt incurred after the date an indebted country first came to the Paris club could not be rescheduled. The debt before this point is 'pre cut-off date debt' and the debt after is 'post cut-off date debt'. The creditors would trumpet their offers of debt relief, but exclude post cut-off date debt. We taught our supporters the difference.

After Uganda came to the Paris club, the British government claimed it had offered a great deal – writing off two-thirds of Uganda's debt. But this was only pre-1981 debt. Thousands of Jubilee 2000 supporters wrote to the Treasury arguing that they must include post cut-off date debt if this was going to be the good deal they claimed it was. The Treasury told me that they got letters on pink paper with little roses in the corner from elderly ladies in rural Britain. They wanted to know how these people knew about pre and post cut-off date debt.

It was empowering to those who wrote. And it was challenging to those who were used to negotiations and deals that went unnoticed. We had to learn about the complexities of international finance, and to do so in such way that we could have coherent and respectful dialogue with leaders who were not used to talking about these things except with other experts.

We were not entirely successful. We have only managed to cancel $12 billion of debt so far. Although the leaders have promised to cancel $110 billion, they are doing it very slowly. And even the $110 million was not enough to restore countries to economic viability. Yet we started something – we built awareness and solidarity.

Evaluation

The main reason for our success in the UK was that millions of ordinary people volunteered their backing for the campaign. Without them there would have been no successes. But Jubilee 2000 did facilitate their involvement. Below are some of the lessons learned by the co-ordinating group.

Understand the issue

The first task for the co-ordinating group is to study the problem carefully. We describe this as similar to the challenge facing diamond-cutters: they sometimes study a stone for two years before cutting it. In the same way issues need to be analysed precisely and accurately.

Look for a strong and straightforward argument (a moral or social argument) that will encourage people to attempt to get to grips with the technical or political issues.

Build a coalition

Use the fact that the campaign has a genuine issue at its core to appeal to diverse groups, individuals and organizations who would not usually work together. We worked on the basis that people could join if they shared our concern for debt regardless of their other beliefs. We found ourselves in alliance with people with whom we would not normally have worked. People in churches found themselves on buses, on demonstrations and in meetings with people they had never talked to before. They found themselves bringing the perspective of their faith to a wider community. If you are campaigning for changes in the south, be sure to provide a platform in the north for spokespersons from the south. Make it possible for them to speak for themselves and to speak directly about their experience.

Coalitions are difficult to handle. Some are loose with no leadership and little coherence. Ours was strong with clear leadership. One of the key responsibilities of the leadership must be to maintain respect and communication with all partners. Allow a thousand flowers to bloom. Be open and inclusive. The core co-ordination team should be made up of people with diversity of background and cultures in order to reflect the full range of interest in the campaign. All individuals and organizations taking part in the campaign must keep focused on the overall mission and goals. Any individual or organizational agendas must be subservient to those.

Support members of the coalition by providing easily digestible information that can be adapted to their needs. This is particularly important for those that do not usually work on the issue. Allow others to use the branding to promote their own organization. Giving the campaign a short life is less threatening to established organizations.

Be 'opportunistic'

Make use of world events that illustrate your case. We, for example, used the floods in Honduras to highlight the way in which that country paid more in debt service than it received in aid. This means being 'opportunistic' and responding quickly to events. Keep looking for opportunities to raise expectations – beyond those that may be considered normal, but which retain a sense of 'just about possible'. This builds excitement, energy and leadership.

Keep the campaign fashionable and ahead of the game by involving celebrities and loudly acknowledging achievements. But be aware of the risks of celebrity involvement. Do not waste their time unless you have something that really meshes with their profile and commitment. Ensure that the relationship is a two-way one, so that they get something out of it too.

Encourage grass-roots participation

Devise easy, specific and non-threatening actions that ordinary people will feel confident and justified in doing. Ensure the wording of a petition is devised to unite the widest possible range of people behind the campaign. Do not use it just for counting signatures, but apply it as part of a wider process of engaging and educating people.

You must believe that ordinary people will be able to grasp and deal with complex issues. Our supporters astonished officials and politicians with their grasp of complex facts. When I starting co-ordinating work on debt for the British aid agencies, I was told that the issue was too complicated to involve the public. When we suggested linking the concept of jubilee to the millennium, the aid agencies laughed at us – it was too corny and too religious. But some people believed in us. We started with an office in a shed on the roof of Christian Aid. With the help of Tearfund UK we sent a leaflet to their supporters. The leaflet described a child in Rwanda who at the moment of birth owed more than she could expect to earn in a lifetime. To our astonishment letters came back, enthusiastic about the concept and giving us the money we needed to get going. You have to believe in people.

We asked people to come to Birmingham for the G7 summit in 1998. After lengthy negotiations with the authorities we were allowed to hold a demonstration around the centre where the leaders were meeting. Then, a few days before the demonstration, the venue for the summit was switched to the country to hamper our mobilization. Why come to Birmingham when the leaders will not be there? It was a low point for us. But by 10.00 am there were 70,000 people in Birmingham to say 'cancel the debt'. The leaders made a huge strategic error. They went to a castle in the country and left behind 3,000 journalists with nothing to do except ask what all these people were doing. The next thing we knew the Prime Minister was calling, asking for a meeting.

Take risks

Finally, be prepared to take measured risks. We often did not have more than three months' funding in the bank. Working for campaigns like these should not be considered a safe career move.

These were some of the approaches we used. None of these techniques, however, would have worked without the willingness of ordinary people. Credit for the success of Jubilee 2000 lies overwhelmingly with these millions of people, most of whom will never be recognized for their role. They achieved this at a time when 'aid fatigue' was supposedly pervasive and deep cynicism about the altruism of voters was widespread.

We live in a world that increasingly seems to value money rights above human rights. Churches are one of the few places were money rights are subordinate to human rights and human solidarity. In Britain it is not fashionable to talk about the poor in our celebrity-obsessed media. Political parties no longer campaign on behalf of the poor. But churches are places where it is still possible to talk about the poor.

Another contribution churches can make is to offer the notions of sabbath and jubilee. The sabbath has been for thousands of years a form of discipline – a limit on consumption and the exploitation of people and the land. A sabbath every seventh day imposed limits on consumption. Every seventh year the land was given rest. Every seven times seventh year debts were cancelled, slaves were freed and land was restored. Our international financial system is based on the premise that there should be no limits on consumption or exploitation of the land or people.

In a world that values money rights above human rights and in which ordinary people are encouraged to borrow money they do not have to consume without limit, the church has much to offer.